CHICKEN SOUP
FOR THE
SISTER'S SOUL 2

Celebrating Love and Laughter Throughout Our Lives

Jack Canfield
Mark Victor Hansen
Patty Aubery
Kelly Mitchell Zimmerman

Health Communications, Inc.
Deerfield Beach, Florida

www.hcibooks.com
www.chickensoup.com

We would like to acknowledge the following publishers and individuals for permission to reprint the following material. (Note: The stories that were penned anonymously, that are in the public domain, or that were written by Jack Canfield, Mark Victor Hansen, Patty Aubery or Kelly Zimmerman are not included in this listing.)

The Bonds of Sisterhood. Reprinted by permission of Bonnie Compton Hanson. ©2006 Bonnie Compton Hanson.

Aunt Bette and the Bed Bath. Reprinted by permission of Risa Nye. ©2005 Risa Nye.

First Pick. Reprinted by permission of Rene Manley. ©2002 Rene Manley.

Grown-Up Groupies. Reprinted by permission of Tessa Lynn Floehr. ©2005 Tessa Lynn Floehr.

New Shoes. Reprinted by permission of L. J. Wardell. ©2004 L. J. Wardell.

(Continued on page 307)

Library of Congress Cataloging-in-Publication Data is available from the Library of Congress.

©2006 Jack Canfield and Mark Victor Hansen
ISBN 0-7573-0551-2

Publisher: Health Communications, Inc.
         3201 S.W. 15th Street
         Deerfield Beach, FL 33442-8190

Cover design by Lawna Patterson Oldfield
Inside book formatting by Dawn Von Strolley Grove

We dedicate this book to those
who have discovered what being a sister
really means. It's not just sharing the same blood;
it's being there as a friend and a guiding light.

Contents

5. SISTERS BY HEART

6. SPECIAL MEMORIES

7. INSIGHTS AND LESSONS

Acknowledgments

We wish to express our heartfelt gratitude to the following people who helped make this book possible:

Our families, who have been chicken soup for our souls!

Jack's family, Inga, Travis, Riley, Christopher, Oran and Kyle, for all their love and support.

Mark's family, Patty, Elisabeth and Melanie, for once again sharing and lovingly supporting us in creating yet another book.

Patty and Kelly's family, Jeff, Chris, J. T., Chandler and Cody, for their love and support.

Our publisher, Peter Vegso, for his vision and commitment to bringing *Chicken Soup for the Soul* to the world.

Russ Kalmaski, for being there on every step of the journey, with love, laughter and endless creativity.

D'ette Corona and Barbara LoMonaco, for nourishing us with truly wonderful stories and cartoons, and for being there to answer any questions along the way.

Patty Hansen, for her thorough and competent handling of the legal and licensing aspects of the *Chicken Soup for the Soul* books. You are magnificent at the challenge!

Veronica Romero, Teresa Esparza, Robin Yerian, Jesse Ianniello, Lauren Edelstein, Laurie Hartman, Patti Clement, Maegan Romanello, Noelle Champagne, Jody Emme, Debbie Lefever, Michelle Adams, Dee Dee Romanello,

Shanna Vieyra and Gina Romanello, who support Jack's and Mark's businesses with skill and love.

Michele Matrisciani, Andrea Gold, Allison Janse, Carol Rosenberg and Katheline St. Fort, our editors at Health Communications, Inc., for their devotion to excellence.

Terry Burke, Lori Golden, Kelly Maragni, Sean Geary, Patricia McConnell, Ariana Daner, Kim Weiss, Paola Fernandez-Rana, the sales, marketing and PR departments at Health Communications, Inc., for doing such an incredible job supporting our books.

Tom Sand, Claude Choquette and Luc Jutras, who manage year after year to get our books translated into thirty-six languages around the world.

The art department at Health Communications, Inc., for their talent, creativity and unrelenting patience in producing book covers and inside designs that capture the essence of *Chicken Soup*: Larissa Hise Henoch, Lawna Patterson Oldfield, Andrea Perrine Brower, Kevin Stawieray, Anthony Clausi and Dawn Von Strolley Grove.

All the *Chicken Soup for the Soul* coauthors, who make it such a joy to be part of this *Chicken Soup* family.

Our glorious panel of readers who helped us make the final selections and made invaluable suggestions on how to improve the book: Catherine Barczyk, Denise Carr, Stephanie Carter, Pat Cavallin, Jennifer Dale, Michele Edelstein, Jackie Fleming, Melanie Johnson, Karen Kilby, Renee King, Terry LePine, Heather Lindsey, Linda Mitchell, Paddy Reynolds, Swannee Rivers, Sallie A. Rodman, Diane Smith, Jeannie Winstrom, Deb Zika and Margaret Zimmerman.

And, most of all, thanks to everyone who submitted their heartfelt stories, poems, quotes and cartoons for possible inclusion in this book. While we were not able to use everything you sent in, we know that each word came from a magical place flourishing within your soul.

Because of the size of this project, we may have left out the names of some people who contributed along the way. If so, we are sorry, but please know that we really do appreciate you very much. We are truly grateful and love you all!

Introduction

When we sat down to create *Chicken Soup for the Sister's Soul 2*, we were reminded of the many times throughout our childhoods when we were forced to work together with our sisters. "Forced" is the word we used when we were young. It's funny how the definition changes over time. In the beginning, our sisters are our playmates, and we don't realize the importance of the role they will play later in life. In our teen years, many of us strive for independence and can't escape each other's shadow fast enough, unwilling to share our friends or our clothes!

Remember the days when you wanted to kill your sister when she walked in from a date in your brand-new shoes? Fast-forward to engagements, weddings and finally having children of your own. Now best friends, sisters are always there when you need them—which is often, whether it be to listen to you moan and groan about something or to come to your rescue at the last minute when you need a babysitter. And a sister knows instantly by the tone of your voice when something's wrong, even though she's miles away.

As adults, it is a pleasure to think back and remember the fights, hugs, tears and laughter we've shared with our sisters. We have been each other's cheerleaders when the going got tough and adult playmates when we just wanted a day off from our busy lives.

If you are reading this book, chances are you recognize this person and are lucky enough to have a sister. Whether you share this connection through genetics or the heart, by common parents or common adventure, only the two of you understand your deep and dynamic bond.

With true stories of women whose lives have been touched by a special sister, this book shows how the bond of sisterhood transcends time or distance—and even difficult times—to allow two people to remain connected. *Chicken Soup for the Sister's Soul 2* will once again celebrate that bond, evoke heartfelt memories of good times shared and remind you to appreciate the woman you are lucky enough to call your sister and your friend.

"You're in the sisterhood automatically by birth, Breck . . . there aren't any bizarre initiations."

Reprinted by permission of Jonny Hawkins ©2006.

1

A SISTER'S LOVE AND SUPPORT

It is not what you have in your life that counts, but who you have in your life that counts.

Rita Fiesel

The Bonds of Sisterhood

Love isn't what makes the world go around. It is what makes the ride worthwhile.

Franklin P. Jones

We're blonde, we're brunette, we're creatively dyed,
Tall, short and thin or perhaps semi-wide.

There's the oldest and youngest, and those in-between;
Politically left, right and middle we lean.

Some have children, some don't; same with careers.
We've traveled on different paths through the years.

Yet one thing hasn't changed, still true and still sweet:
The bonds of our sisterhood remain complete.

As we've each chased our dreams through joy,
     doubt and fear,
We've been there for each other, to comfort and cheer.

So here's to my sisters by friendship or birth:
Your love's one of God's richest treasures on Earth!

Bonnie Compton Hanson

Aunt Bette and the Bed Bath

How do people make it through life without a sister?

Sara Corpening

It was late fall 1999. Marilyn, my mother-in-law, was failing. She was losing her battle with cancer, and her older sister Bette came north from her home in San Diego to give moral support and comfort. Marilyn was seventy-one, and Bette was seventy-five. They had been known as the Burns girls back in Bangor, Maine, where they grew up. Those New England women are made from stern stuff—they don't complain much and usually keep a stiff upper lip. Although my father-in-law doted on Marilyn, there are some things a husband just cannot do. Bette decided that her sister needed some pampering, and I was enlisted to help in this maneuver. The womenfolk were taking over.

Bette started off by asking Marilyn if she would like a bath. When Marilyn nodded in agreement, Bette asked if she would prefer a tub bath or a bed bath. We watched as she mouthed the words "bed bath." Bette looked at me and said, "We have to make a trip to the drugstore. I know just what we need."

So, with promises to be back soon, I drove us down the hill to the store. As we drove, Bette began ticking off on her fingers all the things we would need. "When was the last time you did this?" I asked her. She thought a moment and answered, "Oh, it must have been in the '40s. But you never forget how. We'll need a couple of tubs, some plastic sheeting, sponges, some nice scented bubble bath and a couple of other things."

When we arrived at the store, Bette led the charge, commandeering a cart and checking every aisle. We could not find everything right away, so Bette tracked down a young man in a green vest whose nametag identified him as Carlos. "Hello, Carlos," Bette began in a formal yet familiar way. "Will you help us find a few things?" Bette was clearly in charge now, and poor Carlos was unable to duck out on us until our cart was full of the necessary items. At the checkout counter, Bette thanked Carlos ("Thank you, deah") in her best New England accent.

Back at the house, we sprang into action, donning aprons and filling the tubs, adding some lavender-scented bubble bath to the comfortably warm water. Bette gave me a look that I understood to mean: This will be hard, but we have to keep the mood light—and, above all, we can't let Marilyn see us cry. Using the childhood nickname that no one else would think of using, Bette urged her little sister Mimi to be a good girl and roll onto her side. We began bathing her hands and arms, the warm water filling the room with the calming scent of lavender. I found myself unable to keep the tears at bay and left the room frequently to refill the tubs or run more hot water—unnecessary tasks that allowed me to take a moment to regain my composure and steel myself. Bette, however, never left the room and never stopped her gentle patter. We bathed

Marilyn's feet and noticed that that they really needed some attention. I found a pair of nail scissors and a small brush and gave Marilyn a poor approximation of a pedicure, while Bette continued speaking sweetly to her sister as she gently bathed her and used a soft towel to pat her fragile skin dry. Even though words often failed Marilyn now, she murmured her appreciation and smiled as we pampered her.

Once the bath was finished, we massaged lavender lotion on her arms and legs, the soothing scent working into her papery skin. We kept up a little conversation, calling each other Olga and Helga, keeping things light, keeping our hearts from breaking right then as we cared for this woman we loved like a baby.

My mother-in-law was a role model and a mentor, although she seemed intimidating to me when I began dating her son when I was seventeen. Over the years, however, after I married her oldest child and produced the first grandchild, she became more than that: she was a source of wisdom, support and unconditional love. I will be lucky if I can have this kind of relationship with my daughters-in-law if and when my sons get married. She was a professional woman, an educator, and she had a sense of who she was and how she fit into the world. She was never at a loss for words, never in doubt. I think I only saw her cry twice in all the years I knew her. But now, she was always at a loss for words, her clothes hung on her like sacks, and she seemed so lost and unsure.

The bath was over, and we helped Marilyn into a kitten-soft robe that felt nice against her skin. She was up on her feet, slippers on, ready to go sit up with the menfolk in the other room. Before she walked out, she gave her blonde wig a pat, and I assured her it looked fine. One more smoothing touch to the wig, and she walked slowly to her chair. She carried the scent of lavender with her, graceful and somehow strong despite the strength she had lost and continued to lose.

Bette taught me an important lesson, and not just how to give a bed bath. Despite age and time and life's complexities, the bond between sisters is stronger than anything else. When everything is stripped away and time is forgotten, the older sister takes care of the younger sister. *Take my hand when we cross the street. Don't catch cold. Would you like a lovely bath? Here, let me help you, dear.*

Risa Nye

First Pick

To have a loving relationship with a sister is to have a soul mate for life.

Victoria Secunda

None of us wanted to fight. Five sisters and one brother were trying valiantly to honor and respect our parents. Louise is the oldest and had the most daily contact with our mother before her quick death from cancer, which had quietly taken over her body for so long, but not loud enough to be noticed until too late. Three weeks later, here we sat, six middle-aged children in the living room of our youth, with red eyes of grief and nervous sweaty hands.

"We'll each pick a number, starting from oldest to youngest, then we'll each take a pick, in the order of our numbers. You understand?" Louise was fully in charge. We were taking our pick of Mama's quilts.

These last six quilts of our mother's were something we needed to be fair about. They were all laid out for our choosing. Although not works of art for the most part, they were our heritage. There was a queen-size Dresden plate and two twin-size patchworks, both in good shape. A double-size, double-knit polyester little girl quilt that we remembered from the era of leisure suits, and a queen-size log cabin that told its age by the colors: orange and avocado. Then there was the quilt on my mother's bed, a double-size star pattern of Wedgwood blue chintz and cotton. It was gorgeous. And it smelled like Mama.

We reached into the shoe box one at a time for our numbers, and being the baby, I picked last. Fitting, as I got number six, the last to choose from the bed cover legacy. Libby was the first, and no one was surprised to watch her gather up the soft, stiff chintz and fold it into her bag. When my turn came, the double-knit polyester quilt was left, so I took it, remembering mother hand-stitching the pitiful thing. So much work, for so little beauty! *We'll keep it in the car,* I thought to myself, *for a picnic blanket.*

That was in October, and as the holidays approached, our grief stayed with us, mostly hidden, but popping up unannounced as tears over a remembered song or a phone call impossible to make. We all moved our bodies toward Christmas, even as our minds stayed with Mother in her hospital bed before she died, or in her flower garden, or on her sun porch. Christmas would be hard.

Packages began to arrive, though, and I had to notice that the rest of the world didn't stop in the shadow of my sadness. On Christmas eve, my children have the privilege of opening one package before bed, but on this night they encouraged me to join in. A large box from Ohio had piqued their interest. What could Aunt Libby have sent?

Laughing, I tore open the box, expecting a joke—an inflatable chair or bubble bath buried in yards of newspaper—but then my hands shook, and my vision wavered through a film of sudden tears. Inside the box lay, neatly folded, the coveted chintz quilt from Mama's bed. I buried my face in the folds to take in the lingering scent of my mother and to add my tears. On top of the quilt was a card: *To my baby sister—my first pick.*

Rene Manley

Grown-Up Groupies

You keep your past by having sisters.

Deborah Moggach

What we wouldn't do for good tickets to a rock concert in the eighties: camping out in the freezing temperatures on our aluminum-framed, nylon-weaved lawn chairs, wrapped in blankets and leg warmers for hours on a Saturday morning. All of this for the rush we would feel at the concert as the music vibrated through us and we vied for a view of one of our rock idols. My sister and I were regular concert-goers in high school. If we knew the music, we went to the concert. Those were the days when Bruce Springsteen, Duran Duran and Rick Springfield were filling up the stadiums. My fondest memories of high school are a combination of screeching electric guitars, throngs of screaming people jumping up and down around me, and my sister and me in the midst of it all with our denim miniskirts and perms.

We now have children of our own and have moved on to more "grown-up" pastimes—chauffeuring kids to dance class, baking cupcakes for school parties, dropping off kids at preschool. We may have moved past the days of seeing every band that comes to town, but we do make an exception for Bon Jovi. If Bon Jovi is coming to town, we can transport ourselves right back into the concert-fanatic mentality. Of course, now instead of waiting on our lawn chairs, we wait at our computers, hitting the refresh button until the exact moment that tickets go on sale, and away we go trying to click the buttons as quickly as possible to get the best seats available through Ticketmaster. On concert nights, we aren't as concerned about what we're going to wear or how our hair looks. Instead, we worry about whether or not our husbands will be home in time to watch the kids so we can beat the traffic on the way to the concert.

Once we arrive at the venue and hear the roadies bellowing, "Check one, check two," into the mike, the past twenty years are erased, and we become alive and united together in one spirit. When the band appears on stage, we scream, throw our hands in the air and immerse ourselves in the moment—free, young, alive and invincible. We belt out the words and become one with the thousands of screaming fans surrounding us. For that one night, we, as sisters, share a common energy and bond that will hold us together through the ordinary routine and distance of everyday life.

As adult sisters, we may forget to call each other every week as we get wrapped up in piles of laundry, grocery shopping and caring for sick kids, but when Bon Jovi is coming to town, we instantly make time for that special sister reconnection. As we listen on the radio for chances to win tickets and make plans for our concert night, I see a new sparkle in my sister's eyes. While our kids laugh and play in the other room, we sit together and excitedly wonder aloud what the song list is going to be, how good of a view we will have from our seats, and how we are going to get past the security guards to rush the stage. We are children again, sharing our secrets and conspiring together. We may be grown up now, but we are still connected with a childlike fantasy full of booming music and hip-gyrating rock idols—minus the denim miniskirts and perms.

Tessa Floehr

Bonnie and Jean find that reliving their favorite childhood memories can be a little challenging.

New Shoes

*Recall it as often as you wish; a happy memory
never wears out.*

Libbie Fudim

Anne is six years older than me. Growing up, we were
very poor, and my mother worked evenings at a factory in
a small midwestern town. Not seeing my mother much,
Anne took over much of the maternal support, and she
was awarded the authority to give me and my younger
sister permission to do things. Actually, going to Anne
was much better than going to a parent as she could
award permission, but never had an urge to punish us
when we broke the rules. Therefore, we were a bit more
willing to confess our activities to Anne and sometimes
benefited from her sisterly advice. During those turbulent
teenage years, Anne was always there for me, not only as
a big sister, but as a mother and my best friend.

When I was seventeen and had no money, I thought my
only chance of going to college was if I could win a scholarship. I had an important interview for such an award.
Anne at that time was struggling, surviving on a part-time

job as she put herself through the local community college after serving in the army. I told her of my interview, that General Motors was sending me a bus ticket, and I would get to visit the city for my scholarship interview. It would be the first time I ever saw a city. I was excited about the adventure and asked her advice on what to wear. I showed her my best outfit and how I planned to be careful how I sat so that the hole in the bottom of my shoe would not be seen, but I wasn't sure what I would do if it rained. I showed her how I would stand with my arm slightly in front of me to hide the blemish from my factory-second pants from the farmers' market. My best blouse was a find at a yard sale, slightly faded but still pretty.

Anne suggested that we go shopping, and we took the bus to the JCPenney store. She took me to the shoe department, and we found a beautiful pair of leather shoes on sale. She told me to try them on, but I thought it was just for fun as neither of us had ever owned anything that expensive before. Sometimes we did go shopping together and tried on things just to see what they looked and felt like, but we never could afford to buy them. It was like playing dress-up. But this time was different. Anne handed me the boxed shoes and said, "Here, I'll buy these for you."

"But . . ." was all I could say.

"You deserve them," she replied. "This interview is important. I want to see you get that scholarship."

I was speechless as I knew this was a lot of money for her, and she would probably have to eat nothing but ramen noodles for at least a month.

I went to the interview and crossed my legs so that my beautiful new shoes shone with pride. I won the scholarship and became an engineer. Although they were nice leather everyday shoes, I didn't wear them much because they were so special. I hope Anne didn't think I did not like them or something. Now, after twenty years have passed, I still have that pair of shoes with me, and I just wear them on those little occasions when I need to feel special. It's kind of like having magic ruby slippers when you're homesick.

L. J. Wardell

First Walk

You know full well as I do the value of sisters'
affections: There is nothing like it in this world.

Charlotte Brontë

"In Scotland, the country where I was born," says my
mother, "it is believed that whoever takes a baby for his or
her first walk passes along his or her good qualities to that
child. I want you to take her for her first walk."

Gently, she places my baby sister in my arms. A smile of
surprised delight moves across my face as I look down at
this priceless treasure entrusted to my care. Wrapped in a
soft, white blanket, she smells of warm milk, baby powder
and Ivory soap. I, at the awkward age of eleven, waver
between childhood and adulthood, too old for dolls, too
young for lipstick. My mother's words fill me with joy. She
treats me like an adult.

Fresh snow has fallen during the night, and as we begin
this very special walk, we enter a pristine world of silent
beauty. The dark shapes of the trees against the brilliant
blue of the sky provide an exquisite backdrop to this quiet
drama taking place. Although we live in the city, our home

rests in the middle of an acre of ground, so we are undisturbed during our peaceful walk. I place the end of the blanket lightly over my sister's face to protect her tiny face from the cold. Carefully circling our home, I tell her the secrets of our yard. "This maple tree is the biggest tree in the yard," I say. "In the early spring, leaves of bright green lace tumble from every branch. Underneath this tree the grass is softer and a darker shade of green than it is in the rest of the yard." She moves a little in my arms, and I stop to lift the blanket from her face. As she looks up at me, I tell her, "In the summer we will have a picnic under this tree. You will love the feel of the cool, smooth grass on your feet." As her eyes begin to close, I replace the blanket and continue to walk. The swing set built by our father looks out of place in this wintry scene. The seats are piled with snow, and the chains creak as they move slightly when touched by a breeze. "When you are older, I will push you on this swing," I tell her. I am seeing everything with new eyes as I introduce her to the world.

As I walk I notice a rake left in the yard from fall. Dangerous spikes show through the snow. Carefully, I walk around the rake and hold my sister a little tighter. She is becoming heavier now as she falls asleep. When we first started our walk, I felt as though I was carrying cotton candy, but now the weight of her sleeping body makes my thin arms ache. My face is cold, and I am hungry. It is time to finish our walk. My mother stands at the door and smiles as her two daughters enter the warm, cheery kitchen.

"You did a good job," she says, and adds, "I knew you would." Together we unwrap our baby from her cocoon of blankets, and I sense a deep satisfaction in what we have accomplished this day.

Joan McKee

Sisters Bring Strength

Having a sister is like having a best friend you can't get rid of.

Amy Li

On a warm Tuesday morning, I leave work and drive to the doctor's office where my twin sister has an appointment to discuss the excruciating pain in one of her breasts. Although Gayle insists I shouldn't come, I insist on being there.

Elaine, our older sister, has driven down from Tyler the night before. We aren't expecting bad news, but should it come, we want to be there for support.

By the time I arrive, Gayle is already with the doctor. Elaine sits thumbing through old magazines. We hug each other and make small talk.

After an eternal wait, Gayle appears and breaks the news: The doctor wants her to go over to the hospital for a mammogram and a chest x-ray.

My heart races, but I don't panic. The last thing Gayle needs is for me to get hysterical.

When we were little, I occasionally got hysterical. If

Gayle was having dental work done, I cried loudly in the waiting room. When she got a spanking, I went berserk. I didn't want anyone hurting Gayle.

Today, people throw around the term "soul mate," but Gayle and I are real soul mates, although we often refer to ourselves as "womb mates." We've never experienced life without each other, and I can't imagine having to.

As we work out the details of what is to come, I manage to remain calm. Gayle will go for the chest x-ray first, then to the hospital for a mammogram later in the afternoon.

We head over to the imaging center across the street and settle into the chairs in the waiting room. Suddenly, the gravity of why we are here hits me. *What if Gayle has breast cancer? One in seven women develops breast cancer in her lifetime. I have friends who've been through it—some did not survive.* My throat hurts.

The door opens, and a kind woman takes Gayle away. Watching her go leaves a sinking feeling in the pit of my stomach. Elaine reaches for my hand. *I've got to hold it together,* I tell myself.

Gratefully, the chest x-ray is over in minutes. With time to spare, we decide to have lunch at a nearby eatery. My appetite has vanished, but I order my usual and join my sisters at a small table.

After a prayer, we launch into a conversation about what-ifs. It is a lighthearted conversation, but the seriousness of it doesn't escape us. We talk about treatments for breast cancer, reconstructive surgery and about life afterwards. Underneath the chatter, I sense that we're all in agony.

Gayle must be wondering what else can happen to her. Two years ago, her twenty-year marriage unraveled. She was left with no self-esteem, and it has taken all this time for her to finally feel like a whole person again. Now, this.

Suddenly, I want to reach out and touch her hand. I

want to look into her eyes and let her know how much I love her, and how proud I am of the way she has made a new life for herself and her daughter. But I fear I can't say anything without falling apart, so it goes unsaid.

We finish eating, drive back to the hospital and sit in the breast center's waiting room. There are magazines, and we each take one.

When we were growing up, one of our favorite events was the arrival of a new Sears & Roebuck catalog. What followed went something like this: Elaine held the book and sat between me and Gayle on the sofa. Opening to page one, she would point to the page and say, "Gayle," which meant that it was Gayle's turn to look at the pictures on the page and make up a story about them. Gayle might say, "That's me in the red dress, and that's my best friend in the black hat. We've just been to see the Queen of England."

On page two, Elaine would point and say, "Dayle," at which time I would concoct some tale about the images there. On the third page, Elaine would point and say, "Elaine," then proceed to spin her own lively story.

On and on the chant would go. Page after page, it was Gayle, Dayle, Elaine. Gayle, Dayle, Elaine. Our hopes and dreams were whispered over the pages of a Sears & Roebuck catalog. Now, my only wish is for Gayle to be okay. *Please, God, let Gayle be okay.*

It helps to know we aren't alone in our anxious waiting. In hospitals across America, other sisters are clasping hands, hoping and praying that it will not be their loved one who must embark on this intensely personal journey. But every three minutes, a woman in this country is told she has breast cancer. Truth is, we're all afraid. And it is our fear that unites us and energizes us in the fight for a cure.

A cheerful nurse appears and escorts us through a door. From there, things move quickly. Gayle is taken into a room, the mammogram is performed, and the results are read by a radiologist, who isn't totally pleased with what he sees. Although no masses are seen, there are some dense areas, so he orders an ultrasound.

By this time, I have resigned myself to the idea. If Gayle has breast cancer, we will get through it. I think of all the difficult things my sisters and I have been through in our lifetimes, and I know this will be no different. Together—and with God's help—we will endure whatever comes to us.

After a while, the radiologist emerges from the ultrasound room, smiling. I take that as a good sign. "You can go in and see her now," he tells us, and we do.

Gayle is beaming. Turns out, there is no evidence of cancer, only "normal fibroglandular changes" in the breast. A collective sigh of relief fills the room.

Later, as we walk slowly to the parking lot, I realize that it is in the disquieting struggles and fears of life that families come together and find the strength to survive, to move forward, to cope.

With the sun on my face, I inhale the warm afternoon air, deeply grateful for my sisters beside me. Our little circle—Gayle, Dayle, Elaine—has been strengthened once again.

Dayle Allen Shockley

A Portrait of Love

I can't picture my life without a sister, growing up sharing happiness, hilarity and heartbreak. Our likes and dislikes are second nature to us, two peas in a pod. We have made a game of searching for the perfect birthday and holiday gifts for each other. Some of our attempts have been more successful than others, as my sister once sent me a helium-filled bouquet from a company called Balloonatics. When the delivery person rang my intercom, I misheard him screaming that he was a "lunatic," and I placed a frantic call for help to 911. Another time, forgetting that she had gone on a weekend spa vacation, I shipped a box of her favorite treats, from gourmet chocolates to freshly baked bagels and smoked salmon. Unfortunately, the box sat out in the August sun on her front porch for three days as the contents within melted, withered and died. Finally, after years of "I love this, but wait until you see what I bought for you," my sister became the all-time undefeated gift champion.

Ten years ago, Debbie came up with the perfect birthday gift for me—two antique silver frames filled with priceless memories—and remains the Gift-Giving Queen in my heart and mind. Our mom died when we were very young, and our father left few reminders of her for us to share. I carried one tiny cropped photo of Mom in my wallet, but lost it when my purse was stolen at work. It was irreplaceable and the only memory I had of her. I remember calling Debbie and sobbing my tale of woe to her, while hearing the sound of her commiseration and concern.

This was her call to action, and after months of searching through boxes in our father's garage and contacting relatives for assistance, Debbie finally found two old photos, never telling me about their existence. One was taken on the day of Mom's engagement, posing in her formal dining room: a true pinup-style sweater girl wearing platform shoes and bobby socks. The other showed her on her wedding day in February 1949, as beautiful as a princess in a long-sleeved, heavily draped satin gown. She held a bridal bouquet of cascading white orchids and wore an intricate seed-pearl crown atop her bangs and pompadour. I always think of that photo as "Cinderella Gets Married."

My sister had the small, crinkled, faded and torn black-and-white snapshots restored and enlarged to 8" x 10" by a photo conservator. She placed them in vintage, etched, sterling silver side-by-side frames purchased at an antiques flea market. They are the only two existing photos of our mom, my mirror-image twin.

Debbie knew the one thing I lacked—the gift of tangible memories. She enabled me to look back at the past and into the future. As I gaze into Mom's eyes whenever I am feeling sentimental, the remembrance of our sisterly love and devotion comes completely into focus.

Robin Ehrlichman Woods

The Sister Test

Love is a discovery without end.

Earnest Larsen

It began with my observation to my sister that our beautiful, rosy-cheeked mother was looking pale. I remember trying to keep the panic out of my voice, but I was certainly feeling it. Something was obviously wrong with Mom, and I was wondering whether Ruthie had noticed it, too.

She had.

And so began our unwelcome and painful waltz with our ninety-five-year-old mother's first real siege with serious illness. My sister and I had been so blessed: not only had we had our mom all these years, we'd had a healthy, vigorous and spunky mom to boot.

So this sudden and precipitous immersion into new and wondrous terms like "mass" and "metastasis" and "chemotherapy" was like walking on the moon for two dazed daughters.

Never before in all our decades as sisters had Ruthie and I been as sorely tested. Instead of filling our lives with

family, work and small indulgences, we were now frantically comparing schedules. Who would take Mom to the
oncologist? The pulmonologist? The gastroenterologist?
The next CAT scan?

Who would try to decipher the internist's last cryptic
message? And which one of us would start the "new normal" routine of scheduling nurse's aides when we couldn't
be with our ailing mother?

Mom herself was amazing: unflappable, determined
and still talking about when she could resume her aerobics—yes, aerobics. Just like her daughters, illness was a
vast foreign country to her.

The sibling congeniality lasted for a few weeks, and
then came the truly rough decisions that would test our
bonds of sisterhood like nothing ever had.

Sitting in a hospital lounge on those awful molded
plastic chairs, we faced a curt and cool young physician
who gave us the ultimatum: Mom needed a form of chemotherapy to arrest the tumor that was growing in her
chest, and she needed it soon. Without it, there was
almost no hope for survival. By now, Mom herself was
too weak and too confused to make the decision herself.

Two sisters who used to fight over sweaters and whose
turn it was to use the car were suddenly looking our
mother's terminal illness square in the face . . . and, in the
process, resurrecting old ghosts.

I'm the fearful, pathologically squeamish sister, the one
who hid her face when the little girl next door came home
after an accident with her arm in a cast.

Ruthie is the tough cookie, stalwart, stoic and, yes, stubborn. But rational, wise and strong, too.

"We can't put her through this," I insisted when the doctor outlined the possible side effects. "Let her go in peace."

"We have to consider it," argued my sister.

I will never, ever forget that conversation, which

quickly turned into an awful, debilitating argument. I will never forget the pain I felt about what was slipping away that night, and it was not only our mother. It was also two sisters who had faced so much together but now were up against the one thing we couldn't solve with a conversation and a hug. Not this time . . .

When it was clear that nothing could be settled in that stifling little space with the young doctor tapping his foot in impatience, we decided to sleep on it all.

As we went our separate ways, I looked back once and saw my sister walking down the street with her usual purposeful stride. I barely made it to the car before breaking down in wracking sobs.

The next morning, I knew what I was going to say. "It's up to you," I told my big sister. "YOU decide."

And suddenly, across area codes, I heard Ruthie laugh. "Those were going to be my exact words to you," she said.

And somehow, that laughter was both a balm and a clarifier. Suddenly, we could talk without the awful tension and anger of the night before.

Our decision: Mom would have the antibody treatment, not because we thought she should, but because it's what she would have chosen if she were well enough to make choices.

I suppose, by most standards, I, the sister who really didn't want to subject Mom to the treatment, "lost."

But, oh how I won when after three treatments, Mom started rallying. After four, she was almost her old self.

And six months after my sister and I had faced our toughest sister test, our mom was back to her aerobics class.

For now, we can rejoice in this gift of her dramatic improvement. Ruthie and I keep taking pictures of our mother to preserve forever the good fortune of the here and now.

And there's nothing quite as wonderful as celebrating blessings . . . with a sister.

Sally Friedman

Out of the Blue and into My Heart

She walked out of the Jetway, pushing a double stroller carrying small, tow-headed and groggy identical twin girls, with their older sister, brother and father trailing behind. Except for the blonde hair, she looked every inch my mother—more so than either my sister or I ever have or ever will I suspect. We had written letters, exchanged pictures and a few phone calls, but just like when you read all the books and attend all the classes in preparation for having a baby, no amount of groundwork could have prepared any of us for what this newest arrival would mean to our family, least of all me.

I was sixteen when I learned I had an older sister. My mom had been involved with a married man in her mid-twenties when she found herself pregnant. Being in no position to raise a child on her own, she gave the baby girl up for adoption. A few years later, she met and married my dad and had three more children—me, my sister and brother. She told my dad about the baby before they were married, but opted not to tell us when we were young.

When I first learned of my half-sister's existence, I hated her. In my mind, she had ruined my perfect family and usurped my esteemed role as oldest child. I knew my mother's decisions both to give up the baby and finally to tell us about her had been exceedingly painful, but I felt no compassion, only anger. Instead of thinking my mom had marveled at all the newness and excitement of being pregnant with me, I believed she grieved over the child she had given away with each of my kicks. I felt the special connection my mom and I should share because of my birth order had been severed by a person with whom I could never possibly share any kind of bond. It was a good thing that we would probably never meet. What could I, would I, possibly say?

Six years passed. I had graduated from college, gotten a job and was living a more or less normal post-college life. Somewhat out of the blue one early fall day, my mom asked if it would be okay if she opened the adoption files that had been locked by the courts for over twenty years. She didn't want to search herself, but she didn't want to prevent anyone from searching for her. Fortunately, I had matured enough in those years to take this news much more in stride than I had the initial information, and I agreed to her opening the documents. Still, I was tentative.

Just before Mother's Day in 1992, my mom got a call from the Bureau of Vital Statistics that they had a match to her information, and her biological child might contact her. The day after Mother's Day, a letter arrived. It had been just over six months since she had opened the records. My sister's search had been even shorter. She had only filed her papers at the end of April and was informed two weeks later that they had a match. A scurry of exchanges via mail and phone followed that first letter (this was before e-mail) as we learned more about my sister, her adoptive family, and her husband and children, who consisted at the time of one daughter and son. She sent each of us our own letter, introducing herself. How I wish I had kept mine! But the fear I was feeling over what welcoming this person into our lives might mean—not to mention my own fastidiousness, a trait that I would later find I share with her—did not allow me to. I figured the novelty of the situation would soon wear thin, and once the major questions were answered as to how everything transpired, we would all go back to life as we knew it. Well, maybe we would exchange Christmas cards.

It came as a huge relief to my mother that my sister had not ended up in foster care and that she had grown up healthy and happy. We learned that she had been adopted at three months by a couple who had a biological son eleven years older than she. They had moved from our city to a small town in the Midwest when she was fairly young, and that is where she grew up. She got married right out of college and had started a family soon thereafter.

It came as a huge shock to me that although my mother did not name her, her first name, Jolee, is almost the same as my middle name, Jolie. Moreover, she chose my birthday as her wedding date, and it is in April, not June or anything as predictable as that. We both like to cross-stitch, a hobby not practiced by any of the other members of our families of origin. We share the same love of the color purple and have a flair for decorating. No longer able to ignore the miracles of similarity, my heart was softened, and I finally met my sister.

Originally, Jolee had planned to travel with her family to meet us soon after first making contact, but then discovered she was pregnant . . . with twins. So it wasn't until the summer of 1994 that they finally were able to make the trip. The connection between all of us was amazing—magical even. We had gotten to know each other somewhat through the letters and phone calls, but when we finally saw each other in person, it was like reconnecting with that friend that you don't see for years, but when you do, it's like no time has passed.

They came for the fourth of July. It seemed like no small coincidence that the fireworks display that my family had always gone to when we were growing up—but hadn't been scheduled for years before and hasn't happened since—was on that year. We had a blast watching them, eating fried chicken and ice cream, running through the sprinkler and taking scads of pictures. It was a family reunion for a family really meeting for the first time.

In the years since meeting the sister I thought I didn't want, Jolee and I have grown close enough for me to ask her to be one of only three bridesmaids in my wedding. We have shared war stories of marriage and childrearing over phone calls, in old-fashioned letters and now mostly via e-mail. Occasionally, the fact that we weren't raised in the same household or place is evident in our exchanges, but more often, I continue to discover our similarities. Just recently, I found out that we have the same favorite flowers—pink roses with periwinkle wildflowers.

The word "sister" is rife with meaning. She is someone with whom we share biology and/or life experience; to whom we tell our secrets and with whom (and sometimes about whom) we gossip; for whom we will go to the ends of the Earth. Growing up, I felt lucky to have one sister to share these experiences with. I didn't think I was missing anything. But when Jolee walked off that plane, I let her walk into my heart, and my life is all the richer for it.

Charisse J. Broderick King

Hope Blossoms

Seven years ago, I made a call to my sister that left me unable to get out of my chair afterward.

As I gazed out my office window at the lush summer blooms erupting in every direction, I thought, *This conversation and these surroundings can't be happening in the same moment. Here I call to wish her a happy birthday in her favorite season, and she's telling me that she's just come home with a breast-cancer diagnosis.*

It's probably the worst kind of helplessness to watch someone we love shoulder a burden that demands the deepest bravery—and greatest vulnerability—she may ever find in herself. Everything about this development in my sister's life happened fast, from the discovery of the tumor to the surgery scheduled just a day later. I wanted so much to book a flight and go be with her, to be able to do something.

Instead, I needed to turn my attention to the high-season pace of the conference center where I worked, where forty junior-high-schoolers were due to arrive in an hour, and it was my job to get them settled in.

Then, shortly on the heels of my sister's call, came another advising that one of the cabin counselors for the kids' session wasn't going to be able to make it. The only person available to take her place and serve as sleep-in chaperone for eleven preadolescent girls seemed to be me.

It was a long list of feelings I experienced that afternoon—when I was able to feel anything at all. These included shock, disbelief, sadness, anger and, perhaps biggest of all, survivor's guilt, plus plenty of fearfulness. I also experienced a strange, hollow place inside where I seemed to feel nothing at all. Maybe that's what helped me get through those next hours until it was time to enforce curfew with the kids.

When a coworker approached me excitedly that afternoon with news about an exhibit in which she'd been invited to take part, my response was one for which I'd need to make amends later. I knew her paintings were the release that often helped her find the heart to do the hard work required of us, especially during the summer months, but I wasn't a very supportive listener or friend that day. I was too immersed in the pain of my own troubles.

However, I did manage to do one thing I've felt grateful for ever since: I went back to her a few hours later to apologize. When she heard what was on my mind, she spontaneously offered what would prove a far-reaching response. She held me quietly for a few moments, then promised to pray both for me and my sister. She even asked shyly whether I might like to say some prayers together. I was happy that she offered because I hadn't been able to get to that myself quite yet.

Afterward, I definitely felt better, or at least different, as I contemplated the night ahead, one in which I was sure I wouldn't get much sleep, and after which I'd still have to struggle through another ten-hour day.

I had just been thinking about my sister when the phone rang, and she was the caller. All of the arrangements were in place for her surgery the next day, she told me. Then she surprised me by saying, "I don't know what happened this afternoon, but I suddenly felt a shift that's made me feel such peace ever since, despite everything that's happening."

Then she went on to describe a decision she'd made to plant bougainvillea on the balcony of her townhouse as soon as her recovery was past. She'd seen the plant during her travels in the Caribbean and had always wanted to plant some but had been afraid her mid-Atlantic climate wouldn't support it.

"But I'm going to take the chance this year and see what happens. I'm going to fill the deck with it," she told me.

Within those words, I heard her confidence, even faith, as she went forward into her surgery and treatment. I felt astonished at the depth of hope I heard in her voice. It was in that same conversation that she also told me, "I'm going to die eventually from something, but I'm not going to let this disease have my life—my living—now."

That night, something amazing happened as those pre-teen girls and I got ready for bed. One of them, a quiet fourteen-year-old, had been crying in another room when one of the other girls found her and came to tell me about it. What moved me most was the genuine concern and compassion that all of the other girls instantly showed and expressed for her. It turns out that her mother was also battling cancer, and this girl felt sad even to be away from her that night.

I couldn't help thinking what remarkable answers my artist friend's prayers were already bringing as the group of us spontaneously began a long heart-to-heart that eventually ended in its own circle of prayers for her mother, my sister and all of us. As such conversations do when the participants are youths, this one included lots of questions, and I think that our hearts found many answers that night in our little shared circle. Surprisingly, we all fell asleep peacefully, myself included, and passed a far better night than I would ever have expected.

The next morning, I woke from a dream in which masses of pink bougainvillea blossoms filled up the side of a wall. It left me with a pleasant sense of calm, a shift in my inner numbness, and better energy with which to begin the long day ahead of me, during which my sister would undergo surgery. I still felt some wistfulness about being powerless to help her and wished there was some tangible way to show her my love and care, especially because I couldn't do it in person.

When I saw my artist friend at breakfast, I remembered suddenly that she had once lived in the Caribbean. Within hours, I was in her studio searching through several dozen paintings. Though beautiful, none was what I sought.

Then I asked her about bougainvillea, and she found a painting that had been hidden away out of sight. The image's familiarity took my breath away. It was a view of a cascade of brilliant pink blooms tumbling over a whitewashed wall—just like the one in my dream, the wall near my sister's deck.

In that moment, I was overwhelmed with tears that had at least a half-dozen reasons, but the biggest was astonished gratitude.

Today, that painting's a bright reminder on my sister's wall of the blossoms that did thrive after all, the ones she lived to see and appreciate all the more deeply.

For me, it's a reminder that no matter what is happening in our lives, prayer, and what we can offer to each other, are the most precious resources—not because they make the problems go away, but because they change our experience and our perceptions within them. And they bring the more important answers, even though those may not be the ones we think we're looking for.

Phyllis Ring

2

THE BOND BETWEEN SISTERS

The mildest, drowsiest sister has been known to turn tiger if her sibling is in trouble.

Clara Ortega

Beautiful Flower

We are sisters. We will always be sisters. Our differences may never go away, but neither will our song.

Elizabeth Fishel

I used to play alone in my grandmother's gardens. I could almost get lost among the climbing blue hollyhocks and tall gladiolas. Even though I loved to play there, I always felt so alone. My mother died when I was three. My father didn't have much to do with me. Over the years I was shuffled between stepmothers, my grandmother and even an orphanage. And I was an only child. I had always wanted a sister. I felt something missing, a void so deep, longing for a sister. But it was not to be.

Playing in my grandmother's gardens, I used to imagine a sister as beautiful as a flower, someone to walk to school with me, someone to read to me and play with dolls. Still, I knew it wasn't real.

I grew up, got married and had a family. I worked hard and was grateful for what I had. But sometimes, in the quiet of the evening, looking out over the vast green openness and the multitude of twinkling stars above, I still felt a strange longing for that connection only found in a sister.

One night I was out on the porch in the stillness of the waning day. I rocked gently, working a needle through my embroidery. I stared up into the heavens and felt that strange longing again. I was just about to go inside and get ready for bed when the phone rang. I dropped my sewing and rushed inside, my black Lab, Topper, at my heels.

"Hello?"

"Hello. I hope I have the right number. This is the Springfield police."

"Police?" I asked, bracing for bad news. Springfield, Vermont, was a town a few hours away where many of my relatives lived and where I had gone to high school, but I hadn't been there in years.

"We have a letter here asking if we know the whereabouts of one Luanne Higgins," the voice continued.

Higgins was my maiden name. "I'm Luanne. What is this all about?" I asked.

"It's from your sister," the police officer said.

Sister! I sighed and shook my head. "I don't have any sister," I said at last.

"Well, ma'am, they left a telephone number if you want to respond."

I had no idea what was going on, but I copied down the number anyway. I read the last name I'd been given: Manley. It meant nothing. The phone number was in Maine. I knew no one in Maine. It didn't make a lick of sense. *This must be a joke.*

After two days of staring at that number on the slip of paper, I decided to call. One thought kept nagging at me: *What if it was true? What if . . . ?*

It took me hours to work up the courage. I kept looking at the phone, and then I'd turn on my heels and walk away. Finally, I picked up the receiver. I let the phone ring . . . one time . . . two . . . *This is ridiculous. I should hang up.* Three . . . four . . .

"Hello?"

Now what? I stumbled all over my words. "Uh . . . this is . . . this is Luanne."

There was total silence. *Great! I've gone and made a darn fool of myself. This person has no idea what I'm talking about.*

Moments passed. Then I heard a woman's voice, weak, almost a whisper. "Luanne? Oh, my . . . Luanne! Is it really you? I've been looking for you for fifty years!"

I couldn't grasp it. "I'm . . . I'm sorry, but I don't know who you are," I stammered.

The voice on the phone tried to explain. "I'm your sister."

It had been so long. No one had ever mentioned a sister. I tried to wrap my mind around the idea. Oh, how I wanted a sister. But I couldn't let my heart believe. How could I know for sure?

"I was eight years old when my mother married your father," the woman explained. "I remember the day you were born. You were so little. Mama and Daddy Bill didn't know if you'd make it."

The details of my birth weren't exactly normal. I *was* little—I had weighed only one pound. I had to sleep in a makeshift cradle under a light bulb for extra warmth. I had been told that much. But my childhood was such a mixed-up muddle, any one of my relatives would have trouble piecing it together. And there was so much I'd been too young to remember.

"I used to play with you and help take care of you. You were like a living doll! After Mama died, we stayed with my grandmother. But one day, I came home from school and you were gone. Daddy Bill had taken you away. I swore that some day, I'd find you. And I've been looking for you ever since."

My mind swirled with emotion. All my life I'd felt an emptiness, longing for a sister. And all this time I had one, searching for me. And I never knew. As much as I clung to this wonderful revelation, it still felt like a dream. I needed to see her to be sure it was real. I still felt like a little girl, pretending in my grandmother's garden.

That very weekend, my heart was pounding as I stood on my porch, watching a dusty blue minivan pull up the driveway. I clasped my arms around my chest, as if to keep myself from falling into a million little pieces. The van had barely come to a stop when a tall woman with thick brown hair jumped out the door and ran toward me. My sister!

"Luanne!" she cried. She grabbed me and wrapped her arms around me, and I clung back. Sweet, warm tears streaked my cheeks. I'd waited a long time for that hug.

We spent the whole day staring at each other's faces, looking for resemblances, figuring out the past, looking ahead to the future. I didn't know very much about her, but already I knew in my heart we were connected. We were sisters. Finally, I had that beautiful flower I'd always dreamed of in my grandmother's gardens.

My sister's name is Rose.

Luanne Holzloehner
As told to Peggy Frezon

An Uncommon Bond

Sisters share clothes, friends, rooms, cars, dates—even boyfriends. But my sister and I share a bond we never expected and would never have asked for.

In 1993, during a routine physical, I heard some shocking news. "Something is wrong with your kidneys," the doctor said.

At first, I wasn't too worried. After all, I didn't have any symptoms of kidney disease. But for three years, my health deteriorated, my charts passed from physician to confused physician, and I underwent a battery of tests. Finally, a nephrologist (kidney specialist) discovered the root of my problems.

After a biopsy, I was told I had less than 10 percent of my kidney functions.

During those traumatic years, I began to pray for strength, hope and peace. One night, I even asked my husband, Travis, to pray that I'd die. It wasn't that I was giving up—I just hurt so bad, and I wasn't sleeping at all.

A walk to the mailbox was a big deal. At night, my leg cramps were severe. And food—just to smell it made me sick.

In February 1997, I went on dialysis. My specialist, Dr.

Chary, recommended that I consider becoming a kidney transplant recipient.

At first, I was adamant that no one give their life—or their kidney—to save me. I thought I could live with dialysis, but after I went through the treatments for a while, I saw that the quality of life wasn't really better than what I already had. It wasn't much of a life at all.

I just didn't know what to do.

Finally, I consented to have close family members tested for a "match." But my son wasn't eligible, and my daughter was pregnant. Then my older sister, Nancy, offered to be tested.

I said no. I knew that the surgery was dangerous, and the recovery time was much longer for the donor than the recipient. I didn't want her risking her life for me. I didn't feel that I deserved it.

So Nancy prayed and waited. And just as I decided to have my name added to the national transplant list, Nancy called me. "It could be a very long wait," she said. "Please, please, let me give you my kidney. I want to do it!"

Even now—nine healthy years later—I start to cry when I remember how Nancy explained that she needed to be the donor. She said that our daddy had told her on his deathbed to "take care of Kat," and she wanted to keep her promise.

We grew up poor, and I had contracted rheumatic fever as a child. Nan had always felt protective of me—even more so after our father pleaded with her to watch over her baby sister.

However, it was Nancy's insistence on keeping her word to Daddy that convinced me to relent. So on April 25, 1997, we checked into a hospital in Memphis, Tennessee, and began the arduous transplant process.

In addition to a similar genetic makeup, Nancy and I share a sense of humor. Following the procedure, we were wheeled into the same recovery room and lay side by side on separate gurneys as we came out of anesthesia. We got to laughing so hard about our pitiful conditions that it was painful. They almost had to separate us!

Once we made the decision to go through with the surgery, I just knew everything would be okay. God gave me an incredible sense of peace. I felt like he was holding me up the whole time. It was if he was saying, "You're both going to be okay. I have it all under control."

And Nan and I have always been so much alike—the way we think, act, dress—that I knew her kidney would suit me just fine!

I even felt confident after initial blood tests (immediately following the procedure) showed that I might be rejecting my sister's organ. At that time, Nancy felt horrible that perhaps she hadn't helped me, after all. Making things worse was our knowledge of a recent Nashville transplant patient who had rejected her new organ.

However, my faith in God (and that things would turn out okay for both of us) was confirmed when my blood levels stabilized, and both Nancy and I healed quite quickly.

When Nancy had stomach troubles in 2002, I jokingly offered my gallbladder to my older sis. I feel I owe her so much.

One thing that makes Nancy's sacrifice remarkable is her humility. "You're so grateful," she tells me, shaking her head. "To me, it was like you asked me for a loaf of bread, not an organ."

But she saved my life! I'd lay down mine for her in a second.

Nancy simply says, "You're my sister. There was never a question about whether or not I'd go through with it."

When I ponder the immensity of her gift and the health

challenges that led me to the transplant, I realize I've learned so much. I always was good at giving, but I had to learn to receive. Don't get me wrong—it was hard. But my favorite Bible verse is the one where Paul says that God's strength is made perfect in our weakness.

And now, thanks to the strength of the Lord and skilled surgeons, we two sisters who have shared so much—faith, a hard childhood, a silly sense of humor—share good health, as well as an uncommon story of strength, hope and peace.

Kathy Clenney
As told to Dena J. Dyer

The Best Christmas Ever

Whatever you do, they will love you; even if they don't love you, they are connected to you till you die. You can be boring and tedious with sisters, whereas you have to put on a good face with friends.

Deborah Moggach

Christmas was always my favorite time of year. I grew up with family coming and going all day long.

But Christmas wasn't like that anymore. Now we lived miles away from home and family. This Christmas, I was particularly melancholy.

The year 1995 was not a banner year for me. I had been diagnosed with breast cancer. As the holidays approached, I was nearing the end of my radiation treatments and physically drained. My mood was plummeting as Christmas neared.

I vowed that I would reclaim my love for Christmas and, despite my illness, give my children a holiday they would remember.

I confronted my children. "This has been a tough year

for the whole family with Mom being sick. So, what do you say, let's celebrate?"

My children's eyes lit up. "What are we going to do?" fourteen-year-old Robyn asked.

"I'll tell you exactly what we are going to do. We are going to have our favorite foods. We will have a great big spread, just as if we had a full house," I said.

I reached for a pad of paper from my desk. "Okay, you each get to pick one hors d'oeuvre and one dessert."

Lists in hand, the next day I set off for the grocery store. Exhausted from my last radiation treatment and the shopping, I dragged the last of the grocery bags into the house and set to work. The small kitchen heated up. I kicked off my sweatpants and continued working in a T-shirt.

Finished with four desserts, I focused on mine. For years, my mother had made me a custard pie. Even after I married and began having Christmas dinners at my home, she would arrive with her recipe on an index card and produce a custard pie. Mom finally left her index card in my recipe box.

I went to get it—no recipe. In a panic, I started to tear apart the kitchen.

The phone rang, and I was grateful for the distraction.

"Maureen, why are you calling today?" I usually speak to my sister on Christmas morning.

"I'm going to be too busy to talk to you tomorrow."

I was taken aback. What was so important she couldn't find a minute to talk to her sister on Christmas?

My sister and I were on patchy ground. We had a falling-out shortly after my mother's death three years ago, were estranged for a year, and were still trying to repair our relationship.

To distract us from the awkward moment, I launched into my lost recipe saga.

Maureen interrupted abruptly, "I don't have time for that."

I was stung. I thought she might understand the emotional impact of losing something of my mother's. Not only was she too busy to talk to her only sister on Christmas, but she didn't want to listen to my saga. It wasn't just about the recipe. The index card was in my mother's handwriting. With her deceased, it was irreplaceable.

"Have a nice Christmas," she said as she hung up.

I was hurt by my sister's abruptness. Already worn out by weeks of chemotherapy and radiation treatments, her attitude was the last thing I needed.

Late in the afternoon, the phone rang again.

"I got the impression from our earlier conversation that I hurt your feelings when I called earlier," Maureen said.

Out of the corner of my eye, I saw my husband entering the kitchen from behind me. I noted a dark shape lurking behind him. *Oh no, he brought someone home with him, and here I am in a T-shirt and underpants.*

I held up a finger to tell him to be quiet.

"I was a little hurt," I admitted. "What is so important that you won't have a minute to talk with your sister?" I had all I could do to be polite.

Paul was trying to catch my eye. I waved him off.

"I am going to be hugging you," Maureen was gloating. "I am in your living room." She screamed.

Confused, with the phone still to my ear, I pushed past my husband. There, standing in my living room, was my sister, whom I was cursing only a moment ago.

Paul took the phone from my ear and his cell phone from Maureen as I threw myself into my sister's arms. Standing slightly behind her were my young niece and nephew. I opened my arms to them as well.

I glanced over at my husband. He looked mighty pleased with himself.

The story unfolded. My husband saw a commercial on television offering airfares for $99 round-trip if you flew out Christmas Eve and returned on Christmas Day. He thought I had been through so much in the last year and was so down in the dumps the last few weeks that he was inspired to give Maureen a call on the off chance that she might be willing to fly down.

He said, "Your sister didn't even hesitate. She said she would come."

We spent the rest of the evening in a joyous reunion, and then went to the Christmas vigil. I was proud to introduce my sister and her children to my friends. Paul took us out to dinner, then we returned to our house and dug into "Robyn's dessert."

Later, I fell into bed beside my husband, who never ceases to amaze me, savoring the evening.

The next morning, a note from Santa was on our tree. He said he was surprised to find Jennifer and Nicholas in Tennessee. He apologized that he left their presents in Massachusetts, but left them each one small gift (all my sister could smuggle in her overnighter). The only two who still believed in Santa sat contentedly watching my children open their gifts.

After a hearty breakfast, Paul drove my sister to the airport. Christmas had barely dawned. Two sisters bid farewell amid a deluge of tears.

Maureen said, "We may have had our differences in the past, but we will always be sisters. Sisters are meant to be together at Christmas, aren't they? Your husband made it possible. How could I say no?"

My sister and her children were back home in time to have dinner. My niece and nephew told all their friends about finding Aunt Bonnie with her pants off. And I thanked God that my husband and sister gave me the best Christmas ever.

Bonnie Davidson

"The stork brought me a sister.
I hope you can beat that."

The Gift

Sweet is the voice of a sister in the season of sorrow.

Benjamin Disraeli

I wrapped the fragile gift in tissue paper and placed it in the glove compartment of the van as I continued to prepare for the journey that lay ahead. This journey would lead me to Oregon, where I would visit my sister.

I had received my mom's phone call two days prior, her words imbedded in my memory. "Your sister . . . miscarriage . . . lost the baby . . . I don't know why." At that moment, I felt a familiar stab of pain in my chest. The baby that my sister had hoped for, prayed for and endured months of morning sickness for, was gone. She would have been my sister's third child, a baby girl named Mary.

As I tearfully relayed the news to my husband, our four-year-old daughter looked on in concern and confusion before asking, "Mommy, did her baby go to heaven, like your baby?"

I looked into her innocent brown eyes and responded, "Yes, her baby went to heaven with my baby, your big sister, Kaileen."

Your big sister, Kaileen. My Kaileen. It sounds so strange to say those words, as I never got to meet my Kaileen. She was our baby who was too ill to have been born. She came into my life along with all of the joy of impending motherhood, and then left when I was nearly five months pregnant. How many times have I wished that I could have heard her laugh or held her in my arms? How many years would pass before I would stop wondering why I could not save her, and why she had the strength to say good-bye when I still could not?

I cried silently as I thought of the despair of not seeing my child's heartbeat on the ultrasound monitor, and the silence of the doctor as she tried to find a way to tell me the terrible news. I wished that I could take away my sister's pain, but how was that possible when I had yet to take away my own?

As we drove along the interstate, I reminisced about growing up with my sister, who is five years younger than me. From the moment our parents brought her home from the hospital, she was always there for me, even during those years when I desperately wanted my independence. She was the child who couldn't keep a secret, the one who was constantly "it" at hide-and-seek because she couldn't stop giggling from her hiding place. I spent years evading her with my friends as she persistently followed us, wanting to be included. Furthermore, my sister brought the art of "tattletaling" to unprecedented levels, and I was often on the receiving end of her craft.

My sister was also the one I could always count on to perform in the many concerts and plays I directed in the basement of our home. She showed up for rehearsals, rain or shine, and always helped make tickets and programs for our parents, who were our only audience. She never missed a meeting for the "top secret" clubs that I organized, and was usually the only member who remembered the supersecret passwords I established to enter the club-house, aka my bedroom.

My sister was the one I called when the boy I had a crush on finally asked me out. She was the one who went out for cheeseburgers with me before the big dances because she and I both knew I'd be too nervous to eat with my date. She was the one who stood up as maid of honor in my wedding, and I was the eight months' pregnant matron of honor at hers, four years later.

She is the one I talk to daily about temper tantrums, diaper rash and separation anxiety. My sister listens when I've tried everything, yet just can't get my kids to eat their vegetables. She is the person who consoled me over the telephone as I sat next to a door listening to my children cry themselves to sleep. She is the one I depend on to share the ups and downs of motherhood with.

As I arrived at my sister's house, I didn't know what I would say or how I would comfort her. Although we had both lost daughters at similar stages in our pregnancies, our experiences were unique. Nothing I could say would take away the pain she felt, just as nothing had taken away my pain six years earlier.

I walked over to the couch where she sat, pale and heartbroken. I handed her the gift and hoped she would understand what it meant to me—and how much she meant to me. She opened the tissue paper and looked at what I had given her: a pink baby bootie held on a string.

"I bought this pair of pink baby booties after I lost Kaileen. I hang one on my Christmas tree every year in memory of her. I thought you should have the other one for Mary," I explained.

As my sister looked at the ornament, and then at me, she said, "Thank you so much. Kaileen has a cousin in heaven with her now."

"Yes, she does. She has Mary . . . your Mary," I answered.

We sat quietly, though not in silence, as our four children ran from one end of her living room to the other, screaming as they played. I remembered the two of us running through the living room of our parents' house many years before, and at that moment, I knew. I knew that someday my sister would smile again, laugh again and have hope again. As I sat there watching her hold that delicate pink ornament, I knew we would all be okay. After all, we not only have one angel in heaven watching over us; now we have two.

Melissa M. Blanco

Two Sides of the Same Coin

A sister is a gift to the heart, a friend to the spirit, a gold thread to the meaning of life.

Isadora James

What can I say about my heart? For that's what she is— my heart. In the dark, sacred silence of the womb, before we were born, our souls met and were united.

Before the world laid eyes on us, I knew her. I shared with her my secrets. And she, in turn, shared hers.

Six and a half months later, we were born into the screaming brightness of the noisy world. Puny and weak, we weighed less than five pounds put together. Even so, a battle, staggering in enormity, was waging war for our lives.

After giving the blessings of God, along with the last rites, the attending priest shook his head and watched as nurses gently placed us in the same incubator.

We almost died that first night, but we didn't. The priest stayed with us, and he prayed throughout the long, weary hours where darkness reigned and fear showed its pale, spectral face.

The county hospital in Ellensburg, Washington, became our second home for the first two years of our lives. Jenny had problems with her heart. I had problems with my lungs. During those two years, the staff constantly separated Jenny and me, when they'd find me almost suffocating Jenny in my clinging effort to be close to her.

Then one day, miraculously, the long battle for our lives suddenly ended.

We were given clean bills of health. We were allowed to leave the hospital.

And so our new lives began.

Jenny and I shared everything. When we got mumps at seven years of age, Jenny got hers on the right side of her face; I got mine on the left. In the same bed, we wiled away our time by telling jokes. Though it hurt to laugh, we laughed anyway, because instinctively we knew it proved to be good medicine.

When my first tooth was pulled, the same day in a different city, Jenny had her first tooth pulled—on the opposite side of her mouth. We had measles and chicken pox and everything else in between as we grew up, and we had them at exactly the same time. Throughout it all, we laughed. We laughed because our illnesses, like everything else we shared, were experiences that proved to make us strong.

She is dark, Jenny, my twin. I am fair. She is stormy. I am sunny. We are opposite sides of the same coin. Totally different, yet completely the same. Seriously devoted to one another's welfare, we have a serious way of looking at life, but we also have seriously crazy funny bones. There is uncanny unspoken communication between us. All that's needed to send us into gales of laughter is a raised brow, a dimpled cheek or the subtlest nuance of the slightest glance. At these times, people look at us askance wondering what they missed. There is no point telling because there is no understanding. What makes us tick is beyond anyone but us.

An early marriage of mine went bad. As a single mother feeling helpless, I appealed to Jenny. She came to the rescue. She moved in with my daughter, Lisa, and me, and she helped raise my daughter. In those early years, Jenny proved herself strong. She was unselfish and giving, and she worked tirelessly to keep the three of us thriving.

When Jenny married some years later, though I was happy for her, I felt abandoned, emotionally forlorn, spun out of orbit. It was a frightening experience to feel alone in the world. With her out of my life, I felt flat, as if part of me was missing. Everything became dull for me, without color, without substance. It was then I wondered, belatedly, how it had been for her in the years when I had been married, and she was out of my life.

Eventually, Jenny asked if I would move to the same town so I could be near her. I complied gladly.

I was fortunate. I was just in time for Jenny's first son, Orion, to be born. At his birth, medical complications had me willing the holes of Jenny's weak despair into a strong fabric of hope, along with all the love and prayer I could offer that I had within me.

When complications arose with her second son, Lenny, it was Jenny's prayers that trounced the strong arms of death that tried to wrest him out of her arms.

Today the boys are strong and growing, and Jenny and I, still living in the same town, are as entwined with each other as ever. After half a century of life, like fine old wine, we are blended, taste and flavor, aroma and color, enjoying the fine mixture of who we have become.

But last week, Jenny found a lump. The doctor said it could be cancer. Outside, in her car, we held hands and prayed.

As I looked out the windshield at the snow falling so

quietly and gently as if it didn't want to disturb our silent shock, I remember thinking that having Jenny in my life was something I had, amazingly, taken for granted. Maybe it was because she had always been there. Whatever the reason, Jenny not being in my life was something I could not compute. We were too tied, too welded, too one. Too forever.

With a sense of unreality swirling around us, we talked about death, of what to do after, in case the verdict turned bad.

Her boys would become my boys, the sons of my own heart. Her concern for them would become my concern, she told me.

"Of course, how could it be anything else?" I answered, surprised that she felt that she had to ask. "But Jenny," I added sternly, looking her in the eye, willing her to strength, "you are not going to die. Not yet. And not for a long time, either."

Bowing our heads, we again prayed, asking for grace, and then lifting our heads, we looked at each other in complete understanding, the preciousness of our lives inside the capsule of the little gray car enfolding us like a womb. That sense of preciousness grew as we talked and prayed and watched the snow fall, until, with aching sweetness, it overflowed, spilled, gushed out of our heavy hearts. Twin preciousness. It gave us hope.

"Life to life," we whispered as we held hands, our eyes never leaving the face of the other. "No matter what happens, life to life."

It's the blink of an eye, it's the subtlest nuance, it's the slightest glance, life, and then, life steps through death's door.

There is another side. We know it. We believe it. We hold onto it. It is the secret that gives laughter to our souls. It is the empowerment that gives strength to our sorrow. It is understood between us. Completely.

It is our victory; it is twin sides of the same coin.

God who knows us, who knit us in the darkness of the womb, before our first communication, in the sacred silence that came from his hands, blowing breath into our souls, knew us before the world ever laid eyes on us. He has promised. Life to life.

I hold Jenny now, more than ever. And she holds me. We will hold each other for eternity.

Janet Hall

Pay No Attention

There can be no situation in which the conversation of my dear sister will not administer some comfort to me.

Mary Montagu

Pay no attention to the tears the day brings
Look back on the days you played on the swings

You walked hand in hand as you laughed and you smiled
You'll walk hand in hand when you're hopeless and tired

No matter how bad that day might seem
If you lose a friend or even a dream

The best friend you never even knew you had
Who's been your shadow through good and bad

She'll stand beside you and fight away your pain
But remember, for her always do the same

So just turn and look at the younger version of you
If you had a bad day, your sister did, too

Laura Strickland

"Sissy and I are going to be best friends
as soon as we get the kinks worked out."

Sisterhood: The Tie That Binds

When sisters stand shoulder to shoulder, who stands a chance against us?

Pam Brown

My husband and I had a deal: when we had kids, he named the boys, and I named the girls. He missed his chance the first time when Jonathan turned out to be Jill. He missed it the second time when Adam morphed into Amy. And by the third time, the bargain we struck had changed: he had naming rights no matter what.

So we had ourselves another daughter, our beloved Nancy.

I never told my husband that once we had two daughters, I was secretly hoping for a third. It seemed seditious to have such thoughts, but I did.

I knew that daughters also meant . . . sisters. And I knew that sisters could be a bond like no other for these baby girls who came in such a rush that I found myself happily crazed with three under the age of five. As little time as I had to reflect, given the mountains of diapers and the inevitable sleepless nights, this I knew: I wanted these daughters of ours to be close. And that overused word "close" still had resonance for me because I had a sister and, yes, we were . . . close.

If you asked our daughters, now adult women, what refrain they heard through the cries of "She hit me first!" and "I HATE her!" they would smile and offer their mother's mantra: "Be good to your sisters. They'll always be there for you."

Yes, in the midst of domestic wars and skirmishes, the travails of toddlerhood and the angst of adolescence, I was mommy-one-note on the issue of sisterhood.

There were months, then years, when that simple goal of Love Thy Sister seemed doomed. Personality/temperamental differences? But, of course. There were also times when one or the other of our daughters was going through some crisis or pain so private that no one could reach her. Not even a sister.

But as Jill, Amy and Nancy finally all got past that age of "Who am I?" with its deforming doubts and rages, they reclaimed one another for keeps.

In our rambling old house where each daughter had a bedroom of her own, I'd sometimes find them late at night in a jumbled heap. They had fallen asleep together, arms and legs twisted and tangled, like a litter of puppies. How I loved that sight!

When Jill went off to college, it wasn't just her father and I who descended into a period of mourning at this ending of "the way we were." Her sisters couldn't even step into her room at first. The ghosts of Jill resided in those pale green walls in the bedroom at the top of the stairs. Soon enough, of course, they found their way into her closets and her leftover clothes. But nothing was really ever the same. Our trio was now a duet, and the family dynamic was forever altered.

But I needn't have worried. Our daughters had actually heard that mother mantra.

In their young adult lives, when there was pleasure—or peril—it was shared by our three daughters. Amy's career dilemmas, Nancy's romance issues, Jill's concerns about graduate school—all became fodder for sisterly love and help.

As they took flight, literally and figuratively, our daughters somehow managed to speak to one another across continents and time zones and distant area codes. They spent one summer in their college years living together in a cramped urban apartment without killing one another. In fact, they each maintained that it was the best summer of that era.

But nothing could ever match how these sisters closed ranks when Jill, the oldest and generally the guide/coach/mentor, found her marriage falling apart. Her sisters surrounded her like a loving honor guard. They got her through the roughest times, helped her regain her footing in a temporarily capsized life, and generally proved that sisterhood is indeed powerful.

Our daughters are all mothers now themselves, and fine ones at that. Only Amy has produced sisters—tiny Emily and Carly, separated by barely seventeen months.

So I'm observing new phenomena: brotherly love in the case of Nancy's three sons, and sibling love in Jill's Hannah and Isaiah. And it's wonderful. But I'm eternally grateful that I've been witness to just how special and spectacular sisters can be in any generation. When the chips are down—or up—my daughters seem to have taken my advice about being good and caring sisters to one another.

It's enough to make a mother believe in sweet miracles.

Sally Friedman

Strangers No More

Only the heart speaks to the heart. I need to tell you my story and I need to hear yours, so that we may share our secrets and trust our hearts.

Judy Collins

Being the oldest in the family can be tough sometimes, and I know this for a fact. A lot is expected of you, from making your parents proud to setting a good example for your younger brothers and sisters. Both of these things held true for me, especially the latter.

There are four kids in the Johnson family, and we're each about three years apart. I'm the oldest, followed by my brother Cory, then my sister Hylee, and finally the baby of the family, sister Shayla. With flaming red hair and a personality to match, Shayla was just a smidgen under ten years younger than me.

I spent my teen years babysitting the neighbor's kids, taking odd jobs after school, studying to earn perfect grades in all my high-school classes and hanging out with my friends. I was also pursuing a possible career in music, so I spent many hours practicing. In essence, from age thirteen on, I was too busy being the overachiever, too busy to spend time with my siblings, especially Shayla.

Fiercely independent, I moved out of the house upon graduating from high school. Shayla was only eight years old when I left. While I didn't see my family very often, Hylee and Shayla grew close. When we all got together, I felt like an outsider to their conversations and interests. When Shayla started her senior year of high school, our father retired from his job, and the family moved to Crescent City, California, four hundred miles away. I didn't make the trip north as often as I should have.

Shayla left home after graduating from high school. I kept in touch with her here and there as we both married and divorced, with me bearing two children, and she, one. I eventually remarried, and my new hubby, Ken, and I settled down in a small, rural community just ten minutes from where I grew up. After several years of living in Montana, Shayla and her preteen son, Zacch, moved back to the same area. The oldest and youngest were together again, but we were strangers.

Our mother had fought two battles with cancer, the first in the mid-'90s, then again in 2003, when she had a radical double mastectomy. Our parents' fortieth wedding anniversary was in March 2005, and the four of us kids wanted to do something very special for them. Our parents insisted that they didn't want a big party or an expensive gift. They just wanted their four children together at the same time; it had been nearly fourteen years since we had all been together. This was especially important to our mother.

Cory, his wife, Amy, and their toddler son, Christopher, live in Mountain Home, Idaho. Hylee and her fiancé, Alvin, live in Seattle, Washington. Shayla and I were with our families near Sacramento. Trying to get all of us together was tough, but we finally came up with a date that we could all make. But we still wanted to get our parents a special surprise gift for them to treasure. I came up with the idea to create a scrapbook covering their childhoods, their forty years of marriage and forty years of the Johnson family.

I had no idea how to create a scrapbook, so my best friend, Kathy, an expert, agreed to help. I had lost the use of my right hand in a fall a few years earlier, so using scissors and manipulating small pieces of paper and photos would be nearly impossible. Excited about the project, I e-mailed my siblings, aunts, uncles and old friends, and even called our eighty-two-year-old grandmother, asking everyone to send as many photos as they could. I received over 1,000 photos!

Kathy's husband had been stationed in Iraq, and just as we were ready to begin, he was sent home, so Kathy couldn't help me after all. But she did give me her suitcase of scrapbooking supplies and told me to have at it! I only had a month to put forty years of memories together—one-handed, I might add.

Shayla had recently blown her back out at her job. She could barely sit or walk and was in excruciating pain, lying on the couch, unable to work. She spent endless days watching television and waiting for workers' comp, doctors and attorneys to call.

The call she got from me came with a plea for help with the scrapbook project. Shayla readily agreed, and she and I spent the next four weeks working closely, filling a 120-page scrapbook with our family's lifetime of memories. While I organized and sized the photos on my computer using my voice-activated software, she cut, pasted and used her great creative talents to design and put together the photo pages. We were quite a team!

Shayla and I spent more time together during those thirty days than we had spent together in our entire lifetimes. Shayla was seeing many of the old family photos for the very first time. I told her the wonderful stories behind the photos. She, in turn, shared with me her memories of family photos of vacations and happenings from her life that I had missed after I moved out. We laughed, cried, giggled and reminisced. We became real sisters for the first time.

It's been a year since our parents opened their very special surprise gift as their four proud children and their families watched and enjoyed their reactions. Mom is still with us and is determined to stick around a long time so she can continue to show off the beautiful scrapbook. And Shayla and I are now the best of friends. The act of creating a loving gift for our parents cemented a bond between two sisters, one that will never be broken again.

Dahlynn McKowen

"This is my sister, Louise. The two of us had to triumph over a lifetime of obstacles—five brothers."

The Day of the Manatees

You and I were created for joy.

Lewis B. Smedes

When my only sister, Catherine, was born in May 1959, I was about to graduate from eighth grade. The very day she was born, my graduation gift from my parents arrived in the mail—a large turquoise clock radio. I was thrilled out of my mind to finally be able to listen to Dick Biondi's rock-and-roll show on Chicago radio station WLS-AM in the privacy of my bedroom.

Being a self-centered thirteen-year-old, the birth of my little sister took a back seat to my new radio and graduation plans. Also, the fact that I would have to share my bedroom with the little creature after she spent a few months in our parents' bedroom was not something I was looking forward to. My only brother, Joe, age four, had already laid claim to the third bedroom in our home.

All through high school I had to share my room with Catherine, and after she graduated from the crib, I even had to share my bed with her arm-flinging, squirmy little highness. She was a cutie, make no mistake, and I loved her very much, but being thirteen years my junior, we didn't have much in common except our last names.

When Catherine was four years old, I left for college. Four years later, I moved to Colorado, got married, had the first of my four children, moved to Missouri, then Illinois, Wisconsin and finally Florida. Suddenly, I was a single empty-nester, approaching sixty, semi-retired and welcoming my eighth grandchild into the world. Catherine, on the other hand, lived in Illinois, was married, worked full-time as a first-grade teacher and still had teenagers at home. Our lives had been pretty much out of sync since that day in May 1959 when my only sister's birth took second billing to my new clock radio.

But one day in 2005, all that changed. Catherine came to visit me for the first time without her husband or kids. We were shocked when we realized that was actually the first time we had ever been together alone in our lives. Oh, we'd had plenty of visits back and forth over the years, but never without spouses and/or kids tagging along.

That week we took walks, went swimming, cooked together, dined out, watched movies, giggled, shared secrets and talked. Boy, did we talk! One day, I asked if she'd like to go kayaking.

"I'd love to!" she practically shouted.

Catherine had never been in a kayak, never used a snorkel or mask and wasn't even that fond of swimming. Water sports, for me, were my life. I'd moved to Florida the year before to be in a warm climate so I could swim and enjoy the water on a daily basis.

The next day, we drove two hours north and rented a two-person kayak on the shallow Weeki Wachee River that empties into the Gulf of Mexico a few miles upstream. A couple hours into our glorious picture-postcard-perfect scene, we paddled within earshot of the only other boater we saw on the river that day—an older gentleman who seemed to know a lot about the river and its surroundings.

He was canoeing with his daughter and granddaughter. We could hear him talking about the foliage, the fish and the history of the river.

A half-hour later, the older gentleman waved to us from up ahead. "Hey! Up here!" he whispered as loud as he could. "There's a big manatee! If you hurry and don't make any noise, you can get up close."

Just then the man's daughter and granddaughter jumped into the three-to-four-foot deep river. The mother put on a mask and snorkel and dove under the water to find the manatee. I jumped out of our kayak and swam over to the woman who surfaced with a delighted grin. She pulled off her mask. "Here, you can use this. The manatee is huge. It's right over there." She pointed to an area where the river was a foot deeper and loaded with seaweed and tree roots. I swam over quickly, did a surface dive, and there in front of me was the largest underwater creature I'd ever seen. That gentle giant must have been at least eight or nine feet long and four or five feet in diameter. I swam slowly over to the top of him and started petting his tough, thick skin, noticing healed gouges.

The minute I surfaced, I gasped, "Catherine, you have to come over here and see this!" My sister tied up the kayak and swam over to me.

"Here, put this on," I said as I handed her the mask and snorkel. "The manatee is right over there. It's amazing! You won't believe how big and slow and beautiful it is!"

Catherine was so excited she could hardly talk. She tried desperately to make the mask fit her small face, then slid the snorkel into her mouth as I gave her breathing instructions. The water was over her head, the slimy mangrove tree roots below were freaking her out, and her swimming skills were not as strong as mine. She panicked. "I can't do this! The mask fills up with water. I can't breathe in that thing!"

I wasn't about to let my only sister miss out on an

opportunity of a lifetime. "Then get on my back! I'll take you over to the manatee, and you can just surface dive and open your eyes underwater to see it."

My sister, who is shorter, smaller-boned, and weighs less than I do, jumped on my back and held on for dear life. We made our way over to the manatee. She put her head under the water, then came up quickly. "I see it! I see it!" She went back down to pet the noble creature.

Treading water like crazy, I held her arm each time she went under. She surfaced sputtering, "Oh, my gosh, it's amazing! I can't wait to tell my students about this!"

At that moment the manatee began to move forward slowly. We followed it for a couple dozen yards before it dove deeper, and we lost sight of our favorite sea creature. Later, back in the kayak, as we leisurely paddled around the widened part of the river, Catherine let out a squeal. "Oh, my gosh, there's another one right alongside our boat! It's a baby manatee. Look, on the left side!"

I turned just in time to see the much smaller creature, perhaps four or five feet long, dip under our kayak and rise up on the other side. The youngster ambled back and forth, crisscrossing underneath us for ten minutes before taking off. Catherine and I were too stunned to speak. It was one of those "God moments" where you just had to take it all in. Finally, after a long pause, she said, "Pat, this has been the best day of my life."

I caught my breath. I remembered how smart and strong I felt when I held my sister on my back so she'd feel safe enough to dive down to see the large manatee up close. Then I thought back to the day she was born. And somehow *that* day seemed to be the best day of *my* life. It was the day I became her sister.

Patricia Lorenz

The Bonded Sisters of Hanover

I carry your heart with me (I carry it in my heart).

e. e. cummings

Back in the early 1950s, I said to my mum that I was glad I was an only child and had no sisters. "All they do is fight all the time and steal each other's things!"

My mum sighed and told me that it was true some of them fought at times, but mainly it was a very rare and special bond. My mum was born on the outskirts of Hanover, Germany, and she told me about two special sisters who had lived near her as she grew up.

There was only one year between Sophie and her younger sister, Ingrid, and until Sophie was thirteen they grew up together just like any other two girls. Sometimes they argued; sometimes they shared their secrets. One night, they went ice-skating, and Sophie fell and banged her head on the ice. She was taken to the hospital as she had lost consciousness.

Unfortunately, when she did come around, she had lost her eyesight. Maybe nowadays something could have been done to help Sophie, but this was early in the nineteen hundreds, and they were totally at a loss.

Sophie came home, and everything had to be arranged so that she could find her way around the house. Sophie was intelligent and, fortunately, also a strong-willed young lady. She just seemed to make up her mind that losing her sight would not wreck her own or anyone else's life.

It did immediately make a strong bond between Sophie and Ingrid. Their mum helped both girls adapt, and in no time, Sophie was back at school. There were no special blind schools in Hanover at that time, but Ingrid and some of their friends looked after her going to and coming from school.

As they grew into teenagers, their mum could see the differences between the two girls. Sophie, with all her lack of sight, was by far the most mature and sensible. Ingrid was at times a little irrational and just a typical teenager.

As Ingrid brought boyfriends home, they were immediately introduced to Sophie. Sophie would listen to their voices and to what they said, and then she would either warn Ingrid against them or give her approval. Ingrid soon realized that her sister's judgment was usually correct. By that time the girls shared every secret they had. Ingrid took Sophie with her every single minute she could. They went shopping or to the park or the zoo, and their mum was very proud that Sophie took such good care of her sister.

One summer when Ingrid was around eighteen years old, their mum took ill and spent a long time recovering. Sophie did work for the blind society at home, so she could help look after her mother. In many ways, though, Sophie was limited. She had to get a local bus to reach the nearest shops, and she needed Ingrid with her when she went for the groceries.

Once she had recovered, the girls' mum took Ingrid

aside and said, "One day, when the inevitable happens—
either you leave and get married, or I eventually pass
away—we have to face the fact that Sophie will need help.
She is very independent, but we cannot have her live
alone."

Ingrid was adamant that she would never leave her
sister. "I will never marry. I will never leave Sophie!" she
declared, and her mother smiled but let the subject rest.

Tragically, Ingrid was never to be faced with that problem. Still in her mid-twenties, she began to feel unwell and
lose weight. Cancer treatment was in its infancy, and
Ingrid spent two long, painful years before she finally lost
her fight.

Throughout the two years, Sophie never left her sister's
side. She talked to her, sung to her, bathed her and dried
her tears. When Ingrid was buried in a cemetery a bus ride
away, Sophie insisted that her mother take her there so
she could learn to go on her own. For fifteen years, Sophie
missed only a couple of days when she was ill and could
not get out of bed. Everyone knew the young blind
woman who took the bus every day to go to her sister's
grave.

When her mother died, an aunt invited Sophie to live
with her, and still she made her daily vigil to kneel and
talk to Ingrid. My mum told me that when Sophie finally
passed away, just in her early forties, hundreds of people
from roundabout turned out for her funeral. Everyone
wanted to be there when the two sisters who were so
devoted to one another were finally reunited.

Joyce Stark

The Eskimo Baby

One's sister is a part of one's essential self, an eternal presence of one's heart and soul and memory.

Susan Cabill

My sister Pam and I have always been close. Born eleven months apart, we are what is known as Irish twins. While I have two other sisters and a brother I love dearly, my sister Pam and I have a special connection. We think alike, often say the same thing, look alike and frequently pick up the telephone to call each other at the same time. We once met in Boston during our college years, and when I stepped off the bus after a two-hour trip from New Hampshire, I was surprised to find my sister wearing the exact same outfit I had on, right down to the shoes. Even though I am fairly used to these unique moments, a few years ago, we shared an experience that left us both wondering about the powerful bond between sisters.

I was nearing the end of my third pregnancy, living on a farm in rural Maine with my husband and two small children. Because I had never actually gone into labor

with my first two children, and the births had complications, I was scheduled for a Cesarean section during the
first week of May. My pregnancy went well, and I felt
much better than I had during my first two pregnancies,
probably because I was so physically active running our
small horse farm, spending most of my days outdoors and
taking care of our two small children. During the routine
ultrasounds, I made sure the technicians and doctors kept
the sex of the baby a secret, as my husband and I wanted
to be surprised.

Two weeks before the scheduled Cesarean, my doctor
announced that he was going away on a fishing trip to
Florida and would be returning a few days before my surgery. "Don't worry," he assured me. "If you were three
weeks overdue with your first two, and those labors had to
be induced, we'll have plenty of time for your scheduled
C-section." I agreed and looked forward to the well-
orchestrated, orderly delivery of my baby when he
returned. A week after my visit to the doctor, I had a vivid
dream, unlike any I have ever had before. In the dream, I
saw a newborn baby girl, as clear as if I were wide-awake.
She had soft black hair, a healthy, rosy complexion, bright,
dark eyes and chubby cheeks. The baby seemed very real,
and she looked right at me as if she knew me. I remember
thinking, *She looks just like an adorable Eskimo baby!* When I
woke up, I was still smiling, thinking about the baby in the
dream. I thought about it all morning, and I kept seeing the
baby's bright eyes and distinctive ruddy complexion while
I went through my morning routine on the farm.

Around midmorning, the phone rang. It was Pam, calling me from her office in Massachusetts. Without even
saying hello, she said, "You aren't going believe this! I saw
your baby in a dream last night! It was so real. It's a girl.
She looks just like a beautiful Eskimo baby. And she's
huge." I was so stunned that I had to sit down for a minute

before I replied, "You aren't going to believe this. I had the same dream." After we both got over the initial shock, we laughed about how weird we were for having the same dream, and we chalked it up to just another of our bizarre Irish twin experiences.

The dream stayed with me, but I was so busy with the farm and my children that I just tucked it away and focused on my daily routine. Forty-eight hours after I had the dream, I woke up in the middle of the night with an odd feeling of nausea. Because I had never been through a normal labor, I tried to reason away the feeling by telling myself it must be some kind of indigestion, and there was no way I could be in labor because my doctor was somewhere in the Everglades enjoying a relaxing fishing trip a thousand miles away. It wasn't long, though, before I realized this was the real thing, and after waking our neighbors with a frantic early-morning telephone call, we dropped our groggy children with them and flew up Interstate 95 to the hospital in Portland. The nurse who met us at the door took one look at me and exclaimed, "Don't push!"

At 7:00 A.M., I underwent an emergency Cesarean section under the skilled hand of my doctor's partner. The surgery went well, and my husband and I laughed when the doctor drew in his breath and said in the most technical of medical terms, "Wow! It's a big one!" The nurse took the baby to the scale, and as she reached out to show me my new baby girl she said softly, "Good thing you got here in time. This one weighed in over ten pounds!" There, staring at me with bright, dark eyes was a baby with big apple cheeks, a ruddy complexion and soft dark hair. I recognized her right away. She looked just like a beautiful Eskimo baby. She was the baby my sister and I saw in the dream.

Susan Winslow

Sharing

We acquire friends and we make enemies, but our sisters come with the territory.

Evelyn Loeb

"You'll just have to share it." How I hated hearing those words from my mother. It would have been bad enough to share with one sister, but I had three. And to make matters worse, we were all one year apart in age. There was little that didn't get used by all.

We were raised in the '50s, before it was considered normal for children to have their own bedrooms, entertainment units and telephones. The four of us shared one bedroom with two double beds. Some may gasp in horror at the thought, but it was always comforting to snuggle next to a warm body on a cold, windy night.

Modular was unheard of back then. The one telephone in the house was downstairs in the middle of traffic flow. Privacy was a limited commodity, but it didn't matter much because we were on a party line. The whole neighborhood shared any conversation.

Our family's sole television sat in a corner of the living

room (awaiting someone to select from the array of three channels it offered). In our bedroom, we had no entertainment unit with video games, a computer or cable. Instead, we had one phonograph and a pile of shared records. Those records were played until the grooves wore thin as we danced around the room.

We had one clock radio that served for both entertainment and wake-up call. When one of us had to get up early, we all woke up. Then the rush was on to get to the only bathroom in the house. One bathroom for four teenaged girls? It was a disaster waiting to happen! More than once I kicked the door in frustration while waiting for one of my sisters to finish preening. That solid, old door took a good deal of abuse during the years we were all home, but never budged an inch.

In school, we shared teachers with long memories about one of the other sisters. More than one teacher told me, "When so-and-so was in this class, she . . ." We were all in band, and we had our own little band as well. It consisted of a flute, a clarinet, a cornet and a tuba. All we lacked was a drummer.

As we became eligible to drive, the sharing continued. We had one car . . . and it was Dad's car. That meant we had to ask him to use it. I can only imagine the panic he must have felt when he had a bevy of young girls all asking at the same time. Poor thing, no wonder he went bald.

Joint usage was the law of our existence. Clothes, makeup, food . . . you name it, we shared it. I'd walk down the hallway at school and up ahead would be my favorite sweater waving at me. I'd search for hours for my favorite socks and finally find them under my sister's pile of dirty clothes. My favorite eye shadow would disappear, only to mysteriously reappear the next day. Likewise, my favorite perfume.

The clothes issue wasn't always equitable, however.

Two of my sisters are short, while one is tall like me. The shorter ones could borrow a skirt and roll the waistband to an appropriate length. But in the pre-miniskirt era, we taller ones couldn't wear their skirts. We would have been sent home from school, that is, if we had been allowed to leave the house at all with that much leg showing. They could don our slacks (this was also the pre-jeans era), tuck the hems under and be on their way. If we wore their slacks, we looked like we were ready to go wading in the creek. Life isn't always fair.

The years rolled on, and we grew into adulthood and separate lives, but it wasn't over. We shared babysitting and carpooling, as well as our babies' birthdays and graduations, weddings, celebrations and holidays. We helped each other when we could and worried when we couldn't.

The best of the sharing was yet to come, because in those years, we learned to share ourselves. As we worked and raised our families, we shared our joys and fears about our lives. As our parents aged, we shared in their care and in the grief of their passing. We learned to appreciate our differences and our similarities. We learned to ignore failures and celebrate successes.

We became friends as well as sisters.

Lana Brookman

No Strings

Love is faith internalized and hope actualized.

Robert T. Young

My older sister, Jackie, has always taken it upon herself to be my second mother. Most of the time, particularly during my teen years, I resented her for watching over me like a mother hen. But now, at midlife, my perspective spans forty-plus years of henning that points to one un-arguable truth—my sister loves me deeply. Looking back over the years, I value that unconditional love more than anything.

This truth came most clear to me on August 31, 2001, when I received the type of phone call everyone dreads. As I heard the voice of my youngest son on the phone and sensed that something was dreadfully wrong, my mind raced through the myriad of possibilities of what could have happened.

"What's wrong?" I asked him. No answer—just quiet sobbing on the other end of the line.

I thought of all the things that could be wrong. His three brothers, all grown, wouldn't have called him first if something were wrong. They would have called me. No, I reasoned, it wasn't them.

"Is it your dad?" I finally asked, sensing for sure that it must be.

"Yes," Jesse said quietly.

"What happened?" I asked, a panic rising slowly from a place that held twenty-five years of memories.

Lee and I had divorced many years earlier. We still lived in the same town and maintained a workable relationship. As with any divorce, there were hurts and wrongs and continued frustrations over children that kept a distance between us. But still, he was the father of my sons, and I longed for them all to have a good relationship with him. I admired him for many things and hoped that some of his good qualities would rub off on our four boys.

"What happened?" I asked Jesse again, accepting now that something awful had taken place, probably a car accident or heart attack that he'd been hospitalized for.

But I wasn't prepared for what Jesse finally said.

"He drowned."

I tried hard to comprehend the scope of what happened that early afternoon on a lake in north Idaho. He wasn't a strong swimmer. He jumped into the lake without a life jacket. He swam too far from the boat and couldn't get back. A strong wind came up, blowing the boat farther away. He panicked. No one was able to save him. My boys, now young men, were fatherless.

How can I explain the feelings I was left with? Who would understand the feelings of incredible loss and sorrow over the death of an ex-husband? I had married him when I was sixteen years old. We had grown up together, but grown apart in our thirties. The world gave me no permission to hurt deeply for this man whom I had chosen to put in my past over ten years earlier.

After driving to Jesse's apartment to comfort him, I

called my sister, needing more than anything to hear her say, "Everything will be okay." After telling her what had happened, she said, "I know how you feel," and I suddenly remembered that she did know exactly how I felt. Four years earlier, she had also lost her ex-husband to an illness. He, too, was only forty-three years old.

"Nobody will understand the way you feel," she said, "but I do."

I thanked her for giving me permission to hurt.

The weeks following the funeral, I often thought of my sister's loss. I remember her calling to tell me about her ex-husband's death, and I remember saying, "Isn't it kind of a relief?" What I don't recall is whether or not I tried to comfort her, thinking that surely his death was more of an occasion to celebrate. He hadn't treated her well, and she was always worried that he would hurt her three sons. The years after their divorce had been filled with worries and frustrations. Now that he was gone, I believed her life should be so much easier, never considering that she was hurting.

Whatever this strange pain meant, I was glad to share it with my sister. We talked about it often throughout the weeks, reaffirming that it was okay and understandable to feel hurt when someone who had played such a big part in your life was suddenly gone.

As I started to focus on my sister's life and all that she'd done for me, I began to feel ashamed of my selfishness. Who had comforted her during her sorrow? When Lee and I first divorced, she was there for me, baking me cakes on my birthdays and leaving me small gifts to cheer me up. She called me when I didn't feel well, lectured me when I did things I shouldn't, and supported me whenever she knew I was hurt. Where was I when *she* was hurting?

"I know how you feel," she'd said the day Lee died. I suddenly felt sad that I had ignored how *she* had felt. So wrapped up in my own traumatic life, I had never stopped to think about all that my sister had been through. Before now, I'd always thought of her as this invincible anchor in my life. Suddenly, I realized that she was a woman, just like me, who felt deeply and loved me unconditionally through her own pain.

I look at my sister differently now. She still lectures me and is hardheaded and stubborn at times, but now I can see right through it to her soft side. And I also understand that part of her hard exterior is because of her pain. As I see the years soften her face with acceptance and forgiveness of all that's happened to her, I see my sister more as one of my most significant partners in life, who never asked me for anything, but gladly gave me her heart and loves me—no strings attached.

Cheryl Ann Dudley

The Visitor

I was on the verge of capturing a dream teetering between two states: sleep and consciousness. I could faintly hear a voice calling me in the distance. I pulled the comforter over my head, retreating further inside and letting the warmth envelop me. The images were gone, but the memory of being soothed lingered. Once again, the burning question came to mind: could separation by death really sever a lifetime connection? I had no answer. Then the voice called out once more.

"Honey, come here. You have to see this." The voice belonged to my husband.

"Uh uh," I mumbled, diving deeper inside my cocoon.

"Really, you *do* need to see this," my husband said again.

I wished to be left to the warmth and lingering tranquility. I voiced my objection again. "I don't want to. It's cold out there."

"Honey, you have *got* to see what is sitting on the window ledge."

Jack's a very tenacious man. I finally relented.

"Is the coffee made?"

"Yes, and I saved you a muffin."

The coffee and muffin lured me from the bed, but I took

my comforter with me. All wrapped up, I headed for the living room and my husband.

"What's going on?"

"Look out the window," he pointed, smiling.

"I turned and was amazed to see an owl sleeping on the window ledge. It was white, except for a sprinkling of black on the owl's beak and tips of its feathers.

"Has it been here long?"

"It was here when I woke up."

"It's beautiful." I sat on the floor in front of the window and watched it breathe. "Why do you think it is here?"

"I don't know. We don't have owls around here, unless it is a pet or escaped from a rescue. It may have bumped into the window chasing something out of the tree."

"Do you think it may be hurt?"

"It may be stunned or just asleep."

I thought about that, then another thought suddenly came to mind as I remembered what day it was.

"It would have been Barbara's birthday today," I whispered to myself.

My sister, Barbara, died six months ago after a fifteen-month fight with breast cancer. I think of her every day. More than once, I've found myself dialing her phone number to share some observation. If she were alive, I'd be talking to her right now. I missed her, and I would for a long time. I was still intrigued by the visitor, but then I remembered the dream.

"I dreamt about Barbara and her imaginary childhood companions. She had two mammoth elephants: Tundra and Mundra. She also had a white owl she called Snow. They were in a lush green forest close to a river. It was so powerful, and they seemed so happy to be together; it felt soothing. It left me so calm upon waking that I tried to recapture the dream. It seemed so real, then you started calling me."

"Barbara may have sent Snow to let you know she's all right."

At that very moment, Snow opened its eyes and looked right into mine. For a few moments, we stared at one another with only the glass between us. I reached out and placed my hand against the window, almost touching Snow but for the glass. Its gold eyes bore into my green eyes, and then it turned and flew away.

"What do you think?" my husband asked. "Did Barbara send Snow?"

"Barbara was subtle," I said, smiling.

"Yes, you would've sent Tundra or Mundra," he laughed.

I laughed also, knowing my sister was somewhere laughing, too, and that our connection, though subtle, would endure forever.

Joyce Tres

"Ah, yes—your sister speaks highly of you."

Hello, Good-Bye, Hello Again

We are more alike than we are unlike.

Maynard Jackson

I always wanted a sister. Oh, I had one, but I wanted a different one. The one I had didn't even come home for dinner the night I was born. She was fourteen years old, and a new baby was just going to cramp her style, so she decided to stay over and eat with the neighbors.

I was five years old when my sister, Gloria, deserted me. At least, I felt like she did. She married her high-school sweetheart and moved away. I suppose it was to be expected that she would leave the nest first. As much as I sensed that I was an intrusion into her life, I looked up to her as only a younger sibling can. She moved to a town in the Midwest, taking with her the closeness I so desperately wanted from an older sister.

I begged and pleaded with my mom for a new sister. How was I to know I had been a midlife surprise and there would be no more babies in our family? I spent my days with lots of imaginary playmates and a few real friends, but I was always envious of the girls who had sisters.

The years passed, and Gloria finally moved back to Los Angeles with her husband and two children. I was in high school and babysat for her on weekends. She seemed to me to be the epitome of an Earth Mother, and I was in awe. I couldn't talk to her about my life. What did she know about dating, boys and parties?

When I was just getting married, Gloria was on baby number four. We ended up living within six miles of each other. Eventually, I had three children and went to work while she became the stay-at-home mom to her six. We saw each other on holidays, which were a madhouse of relatives. "Hello, good-bye, I'll give you a call." We never did.

I heard news about Gloria through my mother and vice versa. My mom seemed to keep a tiny thread going between us. I think she was secretly hoping her two daughters would some day come together.

Mom passed away, and then Dad, several years later. Without the "mom glue" to hold us together, the distance grew. A card and letter at Christmas filled in the gaps. Out of sync, that's what we were.

The years passed. Her children moved out, went to college, got married, had children of their own . . . one, two, three and four. I was deeply immersed in spreading my own wings, free to soar in my career now that my children were out of the nest. She was off playing golf around the country with her retired husband.

I imagined her calling me to say, "Hey, sis, finally played Pebble Beach and, wow, it was a blast." During the week I vowed to give her a call, but somehow Saturday rolled around and I never quite got to it.

We saw each other at weddings, holidays and funerals, but it was still "hello, good-bye, I'll give you a call."

Caught between jobs, I started doing our family's genealogy and knew my sister had answers to questions that I needed so badly. I decided to take a chance and call her. Would she welcome me after all these years?

"Hi, Gloria, I don't want to bother you, but could we meet to talk? . . . Well, sure I could come for lunch on Thursday. Eleven thirty? I'll be there."

I circled the block three times before I approached her house. Would I finally find the sister I so desperately wanted?

"Hi, sis," she said when she greeted me at the door. Oh, how wonderful those words sounded. I was afraid that this would be a flash in the pan, a quick lunch and then "good-bye, I'll give you a call."

Once we sat down and started talking, it seemed we couldn't stop. The words tumbled out like rolling stones.

I nearly choked when she said, "You know, I envied you for being the independent career woman." *Wow, she had known what I was doing all these years.*

Then it was my turn. "Okay, I confess. I hated hearing Mom tell me about how you were the perfect mother. I was so jealous that you got to stay home to raise your kids."

Gloria looked at me in shock. "You envied me, and I envied you." We started laughing, cutting each other off as we both started to say, "The grass is always . . ." We had so much catching up to do.

Six hours had gone by when I got back into my car, but I finally had the sister I always wanted. After that, we met often for lunch at the mall, commandeering a corner table in the food court, giggling and gossiping for hours. We continued our lunches and chats for the few remaining years right up to the day she passed away.

I left the hospital that Wednesday with such a sadness, thinking our chats would end. Tears flowed as I realized I had lost the sister it took me so many years to find. As I drove home in the car reflecting on my loss, I heard a little voice in my head say, "Hello, not good-bye, now you can talk to me anytime. I am always here to listen." I carry Gloria tucked deep in my heart, knowing I can still share the secret thoughts only a sister would understand. And I can do it anytime, day or night.

Sallie A. Rodman

3

SPECIAL
MOMENTS

She is your mirror, shining back at you with a world of possibilities. She is your witness, who sees you at your worst and best, and loves you anyway. She is your partner in crime, your midnight companion, someone who knows when you are smiling, even in the dark. She is your teacher, your defense attorney, your personal press agent, even your shrink. Some days, she's the reason you wish you were an only child.

Barbara Alpert

Pots and Pans

"Two more plums," I said to my sister as I stirred the pretend soup in our playhouse. We were lucky little girls, with the finest playhouse on any farm in any county back in 1958. Daddy had taken a small octagonal building that had once been a chicken house, scoured it clean, and moved it to the corner of our spacious front yard between the lilac bushes and plum trees. Mom helped us beautify the interior with her leftover wallpaper, then she donated an old kitchen sink, pots and pans, and a wooden wall telephone from the 1920s. The rest of our home furnishings came from the "ditch," a deep gully in the field across the road where neighbors dumped old, unused items. My sisters and I spent many an afternoon playing house and exploring the buried treasures. We retrieved a walnut rocker, a solid oak table with ornate legs, and a Motorola phonograph with a crank on the side. We chuckled when we heard Aunt Brownie was shopping for antiques, a new word in our farming community. We wondered why anyone would want to buy someone else's "junk."

On this bright summer day, we were making stew in our latest find—a large white porcelain kettle. "It even has a lid!" my sister LeAnn exclaimed when we discovered it.

We hauled water from Mom's kitchen to ours and scrubbed the kettle clean in our hand-me-down sink.

"Won't you come to lunch?" we asked Mom in our most grown-up voices.

"Certainly," Mama said with a curtsy.

Although consumed with gardening, canning, laundry, cleaning and all the other duties of a farm wife raising eight children, Mom always took time for tea parties and talent shows. On many summer evenings, she, and even Daddy, applauded from their lawn chairs as my sisters and I performed plays atop the picnic-table stage.

I plopped two more plums into our shiny new kettle, then added a few lilac leaves and stirred briskly. We spread an old lace tablecloth across the oak table and set it with plates from the ditch and Mom's old silverware. A vase filled with an assortment of dandelions and clover blossoms provided a perfect centerpiece.

"Tell Mom we're ready!" LeAnn announced. "We have stew fit for a king!"

I ran to the house and held Mama's hand as we strolled back to the playhouse.

"We're having plum stew," I said, then added, "Wait'll you see the great pan we found at the ditch!"

Mom sat in the oak chair with missing canes in the seat, and I sat beside her on the bench.

With obvious pride, LeAnn placed our kettle of stew on the table.

Mom gasped.

"What?" We girls gasped, too.

Mom covered her mouth, but she couldn't hide her chuckling. "It's a pot!" she exclaimed.

"So?"

"No, a chamber pot!" Mom was laughing out loud now.

"Like a king's chamber?" I asked hopefully.

Mama shook her head, then in her back-in-the-good-old-days voice she said, "When I was a little girl, we didn't have indoor bathrooms. Instead of going to the outhouse in the middle of the night, we used pots hidden under the bed."

"Pots?" we chimed in unison.

"Chamber pots," Mom nodded.

Squealing in horror, LeAnn and I tossed the plum stew out the window and headed to the ditch.

"Maybe we will find a frying pan!"

Mary Panosh
As told to LeAnn Thieman

Follow Me

More than Santa Claus, your sister know when you've been bad and good.

Linda Sunshine

"Come on. Let's go," Chris whispered as she straddled one leg over the windowsill. The screen was on the floor, popped off with a screwdriver.

"I can't. We'll get in trouble," I hissed back.

"So what! It'll be fun," she said.

And just like that, I stuck my long, lean twelve-year-old legs through the open window and followed her into the night.

She thought it would be cool to walk in the desert. Of course, we were barefoot and foolish.

"Won't there be scorpions out there?" I asked her.

"Probably, but don't worry about it." She was three years older than me and much smarter. Her brown hair swung past her shoulders as she ran off into the inky blackness. "Come on. I know about a party we can go to."

We made our way to the main highway. After a while, we met up with some of Chris's friends, and we walked for what seemed like forever. Finally, we saw a light. It came closer and closer until we made out headlights on a car. But this wasn't just any car; this was a police car.

"Hey, kids," he barked when he got out of his cruiser. "What are you doing out here in the middle of the night?"

"Nothin', Officer," Chris said. "Just walkin'."

"Well, stay off the highway. I don't want to have to shovel you off the road tomorrow morning." Then he took off.

We moved over to the sandy desert. It wasn't hot like during the day, but still I worried about those scorpions I'd seen when Daddy was working on his car in the driveway. We never did find the party, and when we finally snuck back in through our bedroom window, we fell into bed and slept almost the whole next morning.

I wasn't used to doing the wrong things. I was always the good little girl—the one whom Mommy counted on to take care of our little brother. He was ten years younger than me, so Mom picked me to watch him after school and take him with me to the park. When I did get away from my babysitting chores, my older sister was eager to show me what kind of a life I was missing. And, boy, did she!

"Let's meet Marvin and Robbie. They're at Pickle Pond building a raft," she said one Saturday afternoon. "Bye, Mom. We're going over to a friend's house for a while," she yelled over her shoulder.

"Be back in time for dinner," Mom answered back.

"What's Pickle Pond?" I said when we were outside.

"It's across the street from the liquor store. There's a bunch of water there from the rain, and we're going to build a raft to float on."

"Cool," I replied.

When we got there, Marvin and Robbie had already roped together some logs and put a board on top of it. We climbed on, and the boys rowed us out to the middle. The water looked really deep. It wasn't, I knew, but still I was afraid we were doing something we shouldn't be doing.

"You kids get off that raft!"

It was the owner of the liquor store.

"Get out of here right now. This is private property! Beat it, or I'll call the cops."

Marvin and Robbie rowed us to the other side of the pond and we jumped off, getting our feet and the bottom part of our legs soaking wet. Laughing, we all dashed into the bushes, running as fast as we could.

"Man, that was close," Robbie said.

"What are we going to tell Mom when she sees our wet clothes?" I asked Chris under my breath.

"Don't worry about it. We'll put our pants in the washer as soon as we get home. She'll never know," Chris whispered back.

That was my big sis; she knew just what to do about everything. And I followed right along. Like the time we jumped off the roof into the swimming pool.

"Run really fast and push off hard so you make it past the shallow end," Chris instructed.

"I don't think I can do this." I was shaking in my bare feet, my shorts and tank top covering my thin body. Then all of a sudden I was airborne, jumping off the roof and making a big splash into the pool.

"I did it! I made it!" I cried.

High-fives were passed around between my sister and the friends we had over that day. Lucky for me, I didn't break anything. Not much later, our parents came home. We never said a word about what we did.

When I think back on it, all of that stuff could have really gotten us in trouble or hurt us really badly. But the funny thing is, she taught me some real life lessons along the way—like not always staying on the safe side, but taking risks. When I got older, I took college courses to earn my GED after leaving high school early. I stuck my neck out for a new job. I asked for a raise.

Now when I look over at Chris at holiday dinners, we share those special memories, forged by the bonds of a little sister who just wanted to follow along. And when our pain-in-the-butt brother pipes up with, "Did you guys ever tell Mom and Dad about the time you . . . ?" we just look at each other and smile.

One late night, when we were washing the dishes, Chris said, "I got you in a lot of trouble when we were growing up."

"Yeah, but it was worth it." I reached out my hand, palm facing hers, and we shared a high-five.

"Some day you're going to have kids of your own, you know. And they just might have a big sister like me," Chris said.

"Nope, not me. I'm having boys."

B. J. Taylor

A Light in the Woods

I had nearly forgotten the sheer delight of capturing lightning bugs with my brother and sister, but one sticky night this summer, I remembered. A flicker of golden yellow darting through the pines rekindled in me a childhood memory that had smoldered, one that had regrettably almost been extinguished.

The children and I had been out, and as we pulled into the driveway, darkness was upon us. I was fumbling through my purse frantically searching for house keys when my son called out, "Look, Mama! I see a light in the woods!"

I glanced up, but all I saw were trees silhouetted in the moonlight.

"I see it, too!" squealed my daughter. "Look, Mama, over there in the pine trees."

From the corner of my eye, I caught an ever-so-brief glimpse of golden light. I slipped on my glasses and peered into the darkness. Once again, there was a momentary flicker, and with that instantaneous spark, I remembered.

Though some call them fireflies, in the South we referred to them as lightning bugs. Every child knew they were a sure sign of summer's encroachment. My brother, sister and I eagerly anticipated their arrival, for that meant school was coming to a close, and bedtime would soon be negotiable. After the first sporadic sightings, we prepared for the deluge of lightning bugs that would follow in the coming days. We rummaged through cabinets in search of mason jars with lids through which Mama or Daddy, who possessed infinite wisdom and skill, punched holes. It was vital that the holes be the proper size. They had to be large enough to allow air to get in, but small enough to keep the tiny creatures from escaping once caught.

After supper, we rushed outside. While Mama and Daddy pulled weeds or watered grass in the waning light, we played the games of our childhood: Red Light, Green Light, hide-and-seek, or Mother, May I? So caught up would we be in our frolicking that we would forget our true pursuit until Mama or Daddy called out, "I just saw a lightning bug!"

All games ceased. My siblings and I would grab our jars, and the chase was on. We would race toward every flicker, screaming excitedly whenever we caught one of the delightful creatures.

"I got one!"

"There's one over there!"

"Mama! Help me! They're gettin' out every time I try to put another one in!"

Finally, when darkness enveloped us, and the songs of crickets and frogs reverberated, Mama and Daddy would call us to the porch where they had long since retreated. Hot and sweaty, we would trudge over and sit on the steps to count our lightning bugs. As moths fluttered around the porch light, we would discuss who had the most and brightest, then beg Mama and Daddy to turn off the light so that the only illumination would be from our jars full of lightning bugs. We'd sit spellbound, watching those amazing creatures flicker on and off. Each of us had our own theory of the origin of the momentary burst of light. No hypothesis was based on scientific fact, just a child's imaginative thinking. Finally, Mama would say it was time for baths, and my brother, sister and I instinctively knew that the time had come to let them go. We'd unscrew the lids and, on the count of three, open them wide. Streams of light would escape as the lightning bugs scattered, their silent, flittering wings dancing into the darkness. Too exhausted to chase, we would simply immerse ourselves in the spectacle.

Time and age inevitably altered the games my brother, sister and I played. There came a year for each one of us when we were no longer awed by the insect's ability to cast a golden light. Eventually, we failed to notice the lightning bugs at all.

Now, the memory of chasing lightning bugs with my brother and sister was illuminated in my mind as brightly as the creature's flash, and I shared it with my own children as we sat in the car. My son, knowing of my aversion to insects, was not convinced that I had ever elected to touch a bug and questioned the authenticity of my recollection.

"Did you really touch 'em, Mama?" he asked suspiciously.

"You bet I did. I caught more than your uncle and aunt put together," I bragged.

"So," he continued, gazing into the darkness where lightning bugs flickered and tempted, "can we catch lightning bugs, too?"

"Please, Mama? Can we catch them like ya'll used to do when you were a little girl?" begged my daughter.

And we did.

Terri Duncan

In Trouble, but Worth It!

You can go back and have what you like if you remember it well enough.

Richard Llewellyn

I was eleven when I snuck away to sit on top of the world. It was late summer, 5:00 A.M., still dark outside. My parents and four sisters were still asleep.

Quietly to the kitchen I creeped, opened the refrigerator, and pulled out the goodies I needed to make a lunch that I packed in a big brown grocery bag, along with a thermos of milk.

To go anywhere without permission from my parents was a real no-no. But I had a strong desire to do so. I found a piece of paper and a pencil and wrote a note for Mom and Dad, saying not to worry, that I was just going to spend a day by myself and would return by dinnertime.

Just when I was ready to slowly and carefully open the squeaky back door, my second-to-youngest sister, Lisa, scared the dickens out of me when she appeared behind me and said, "What are you doing?"

After nearly jumping up through the ceiling, I whispered

firmly, "Shhhhhh, be quiet! Don't wake up anybody!"

With puzzled eyes and a soft whisper, she asked, "Where are you going?"

I continued whispering, "Mom and Dad won't let me go to camp, so I am going to find my own camp today to enjoy."

"Oh, take me with you," Lisa pleaded. "Please, take me with you!"

"No!" I replied adamantly. "When Mom and Dad find me gone and when I return later today, I will be in big trouble! And you are only seven, way too young to go to camp!"

"I am not too young!" Lisa snapped. "I want to go! If you don't take me with you, I will wake up Mom and Dad right now and tell them what you are up to."

Little sister won. I took Lisa with me after helping her make some peanut butter and jelly sandwiches. We added more chips and apples to the bag and snuck out the squeaky door without anyone hearing us.

The previous day, I had noticed on the way back from school, in a distant desert, that bulldozers were leveling a large parcel of land for future homes, and in so doing, they had pushed a lot of excess dirt into a huge pile. At eleven years of age, it seemed to me a high mountain. And this mountain was calling to me, saying it was a nice place for a day camp, especially on a Saturday because the bulldozing crew would have the day off.

Lisa and I arrived, climbed the high dusty mountain in our white patent leather shoes and white lace socks, wearing dresses, too. Back then, that's all little girls wore. I remember thinking that Mom and Dad were going to be really upset with us for ruining our shoes and socks, but we continued climbing.

Mom and Dad had raised us to be ladies. Tasting dirt as it spiraled in the air and getting dirty, along with fingernails embedded with dirt, was new to Lisa and me, but we were enjoying every minute of our exciting adventure. After all, isn't that what camp is all about?

As we crawled and groped our way carefully up this very steep mountain, arriving at the top and sitting down to catch our breath, lo and behold, we noticed a magnificent bright yellow sun had risen among pink clouds.

We just sat there in total awe, with dirty faces, hands, dresses, shoes and socks, not a word spoken, and we stared at the glorious sun and sky for the longest time. I turned to Lisa, smiled and said, "We're on top of the world."

She turned to me, her beautiful aqua green eyes shimmering vividly, and with a smile on her face, she replied, "It sure feels like we're sitting on top of the world."

About two hours after Lisa and I had talked and played on our mountain high, experiencing our own day camp, and just when we had finished our lunch, we noticed our dad below, at the foot of the mountain. It didn't take him long to find us, and we certainly did get into a lot of trouble—mainly because Mom and Dad had worried about us so much. After Mom's long lecture, we were sent to our rooms and grounded for a couple of weeks.

It was worth it all, though. Life is memories in the making, and even though Lisa is no longer with us, I am ever so grateful every time I recall this precious memory of life with her—the day of our great adventure while we sat and played on our mountain high.

Sometimes I feel Lisa, especially when I view a large dirt hill, a bright yellow sun or pink clouds. And somehow in the spirit of all this, I know that she is on up ahead, sitting on top of the world, looking down at me from her own very special mountain high. Sometimes I see her wearing white lace socks and patent leather shoes, waiting and holding a brand-new pair for me.

That late summer day, I'm so glad I decided to take my little sister Lisa with me. Our adventure, the memory, is heavenly, in more ways than one.

Sharon McElroy

Lost: One Bra; Found: One Sister

After a year Down Under, my husband, Don, and I, and our toddler son, had just arrived in New York City on our way back to the Midwest and home. My sister Betty, who lived in Princeton, New Jersey, had promised to meet us.

"There she is!" I shouted. Even though I was loaded down with suitcases, diaper bags and a wiggly one-year-old, we managed to rush almost as fast toward her as she did toward us.

"You made it!" she squealed as we awkwardly group-hugged, made even more awkward by my six-months-pregnant tummy. "And what a beautiful baby!"

We could hardly stop hugging and kissing. "It's been so long!" I sniffled. "I've missed you so much!" Looking around for my nieces, I asked, "Where're the girls?"

"Home with their daddy. Here, let's get through Customs and head back to Jersey so you can see them for yourself."

We all talked a mile a minute all the way to Princeton. Betty, her professor husband and young daughters had only been back in the States two weeks themselves after several months in Europe. She had to hear all about

Australia, and we had to hear all about her travels.

"We're still living out of suitcases," she explained. "In fact, as soon as we get home, I've got to run over to the laundry building to do a load of laundry. Then I'll pop something on the stove for dinner."

After reintroducing us to her little girls (who scarcely remembered their long-lost relatives), Betty headed for the staff laundry room with her bags of dirty clothes. While she was gone, Don and I had a great reunion with our brother-in-law and adorable nieces. Soon, my sister returned. A gourmet cook, in no time she produced a feast practically out of thin air for her starving guests. After dishes, my own little one was ready for a bottle and bed.

Betty glanced at the clock. "The clothes should be ready to put in the dryer now. Want to come along?"

We hugged and talked all the way to the laundry building. I thought back through the years, before marriage and children. Growing up, we two argued and bickered and competed and never seemed to have a thing in common except parents, siblings and a bedroom. In fact, we were so different that Betty used to tease me that we weren't really even related. Not until our college years did we finally learn to appreciate each other.

Then came the years of marriage and motherhood and living half a continent away from each other. Now, here we were together again at last, relishing every precious moment of it. Yet somehow, something was missing. We were still distant, on our best behavior, "company." Not buddies. Not sisters.

At the laundry room, Betty checked the machines. "Good, they're done. Want to help me put them in the dryers? Then we can grab a soda from the machine over there and sit back and wait for them to finish. The guys can babysit." Sympathetically, she remarked, "I'm sure you're exhausted, with one baby and another on the way."

We relaxed and talked about her little girls, my little boy and my upcoming baby. Suddenly, she asked, "What's that smell?"

We both jumped up and rushed to one of the dryers. As we opened the door, smoke billowed out. "Oh, no!" Betty wailed. "That was my underwear! It's ruined. Every bit of it!"

Near tears, she held up the scorched remains of a bra, melted to less than half its former size. Then she giggled. "Hey, I'll just go without a bra then, so there!"

Giggling also, I grabbed it and put it on her head. "Or use it for a headband." Next I held it up against my roly-poly tummy. "Or maybe I could wear it for a belt." At that, we held each other, horse-laughing until we literally cried.

And there in that smoke-filled, drab little laundry room, with a basket of ruined laundry, we found our long-lost sisterhood. That was over forty years ago. We're still best friends.

Best friends and sisters.

Bonnie Compton Hanson

"I love when you visit! You bring out my best laughs."

Curly Cue

Like most little girls, my sister, Jenny, and I liked to play dolls. We would play for hours, making up stories about how each one would lead their pretend lives. I always picked out their outfits and dressed them; Jenny always did their hair. She loved arranging their hair, especially if the doll had curls. She styled them into ponytails, buns, bouffants and braids. One particular doll had long, thick, curly tresses, and it was Jenny's favorite. Little ringlets of tiny golden strands would bounce while we played. With Jenny's childhood imagination, she appropriately named our special doll Curly Cue.

Our baby doll had big blue eyes framed with perfect, adorable, winglike lashes. Her face looked a lot like Jenny's except that Jenny's hair was straight . . . ruler straight. Attempting to give it fullness, Mom shaped Jenny's hair into a bowl cut and bangs. It complimented her face, but Jenny was desperate for wavy curls. She wanted them about as much as she wanted anything.

Mom tried clipping, crimping, rolling and scrunching Jenny's hair, but nothing kept the Midwest humidity from destroying any semblance of style. Exasperated, Jenny even went so far one day as to cut the curls of an old doll and tape them to her head. She looked ridiculous, a silly girl, and Mom was angry.

After that, Mom sat her down and explained that she must accept herself and make the most of it. Soon, Jenny learned to live with her lifeless hair, but continued to admire anyone with curls. Determined to at least be in fashion, she wore her hair long and straight in the '60s. In the '80s, she was thrilled with trendy perms.

Years zoomed by, and our lives took separate paths. I stayed close to home, devoting my efforts to having babies and managing a home. Overwhelmed with ambition, Jenny chose the corporate life. "Acquisitions," "due diligence" and the "bottom line" were her common catch phrases. Along with her aspirations, she developed a reserve that I couldn't penetrate. We got together on holidays and for occasional visits, but driven by her career, Jenny's work held her heart hostage. She bustled in and out, always in a hurry. Our conversations were random; our childhood was gone.

During the '90s, our darling baby-boomer generation was struck by cancer. The epidemic invaded my community, and friends developed a number of varieties. Even children were being diagnosed with the insidious disease.

I was doing laundry one day when I received an unusual call from Jenny. She was panic-stricken. On a business trip in some exotic locale, she had discovered a lump that same morning while showering. Subsequent tests revealed it was indeed a dreaded malignancy.

Like many families faced with a medical challenge, we rallied together.

Side by side, we went through all the hopes and disappointments. She went through endless procedures, the agony of treatment, and invariably her hair fell out.

Jenny tried to take it in stride, making fun of herself. "Maybe I wished for it to all fall out one too many times," she mentioned one day with a sigh. She started wearing hats. Some were attractive, but we all knew what was beneath them—ugly clumps and uneven growth. She carried on her work this way, but Jenny was changing. She wasn't consumed by her job anymore. Time and again, her business brought her to my town, and she actually had free time.

During the months she kept her head covered, her hair began to grow back. One day, I spied her head without a hat. Jenny's hair was different. Was it the color or the texture? It had a little personality. It was fuller, not so straight. Miraculously, little waves began to form. After a while, I noticed the more her hair grew, the more it curled.

It didn't take long before everybody was admiring her gorgeous curly locks, and I was calling her Curly Cue.

Today, we play like little girls again. Inhaling her presence, I delight in the rhythm of our days. She dresses herself; I happily do her hair. All pretensions are gone; only hopeful thoughts echo between us. Each stroke of my brush reaffirms our affection. And Jenny was right—she looks terrific in curls.

Vivian Eisenecher

Sunburns and Seashells

Sisters share the scent and smells, the feel of a common childhood.

Pam Brown

It was the summer of 1960 when my older sister invited me to take a vacation trip with her to Galveston, Texas—just the two of us. I was fifteen years old and had never seen the ocean. What could be better?

Jerlene and I packed the car on a Saturday morning and headed south. It took us two days and nights to get to Galveston. After finding a motel, we hit the beach. If ever there was love at first sight, it happened the minute I saw the ocean. I spent the afternoon in the water letting the waves lift me off my feet and put me back down with a splash while feeling the sand slip from under my feet and back out to the sea.

Unlike me, Jerlene chose the sandy beach instead of the water, lying on a towel, soaking up the sun. She came for relaxation. I came for fun. Our first night out, we had Chinese food—something totally foreign to me since I lived in a little farming community, far from exotic restaurants and fast food. The next day I was introduced to pizza. I loved it!

I loved everything about the trip. Then suddenly, Jerlene became disoriented at a souvenir shop. She grabbed my arm, and I managed to help her out the door. We made it to the motel where she discovered that her afternoon at the beach had left her with a severe sunburn. She was so ill that she spent the rest of her vacation in bed.

Each day I would gently rub her parched skin with medication, then pick up food at the motel restaurant to take back to the room where we ate each meal. It was hardly a dream vacation, at least not for Jerlene. I kept the ice bucket filled and soft drinks on hand and read magazines to her as she lay on the bed with only a sheet covering her severely burned body. Though I could hardly stand to see her suffer, I truly didn't mind spending time at the motel. Our home didn't have a lot of modern amenities, so a hot shower, air conditioning and even a sink with running water were luxuries to me.

On our last night in Galveston, Jerlene and I walked to an ocean pier where we purchased glass wind chimes that tinkled in the evening breeze. The next day we started home, but the sun coming through the windshield proved too painful on her exposed skin, so we spent the afternoon at a movie theater and traveled at night.

When we arrived home, my mother took over Jerlene's care while I relayed all the exciting details of my trip to my anxiously waiting girlfriends. Strangely, I never felt like I was cheated out of an adventure because we didn't go more places or do more things in Galveston. In fact, that trip was the highlight of my summer. I had seashells from my day at the beach, a wind chime from the ocean pier and memories of foods none of my friends had ever tasted.

But my greatest memory was spending time with my

sister, just the two of us talking, laughing and even crying together. With ten years separating our ages, we were both about to plunge into different seasons of our lives. She was soon to be married, and I was on the threshold of dating. On that trip we shared hopes, dreams, secrets and promises that would last a lifetime. And I saw the ocean for the first time!

Louise Tucker Jones

Amanda's Birthday

Whatever you do, work at it with all your heart.

Colossians 3:23

"You make me young again," Amanda said when we were driving home from the movies with our sister-in-law, Judy. We had just enjoyed a girls' day out. The three of us occasionally went to the movies and then to Ang-gio's for pizza. Amanda had Down's syndrome and lived with my parents in Michigan's remote eastern Upper Peninsula. The closest movie theater was in Sault Ste. Marie, better known to locals as "The Soo," which was an hour from their home.

"We make you young again? What are you talking about? You're only thirty-three!" I looked at her in the rearview mirror. She was sitting in the back seat with her tan and navy raincoat on, her wig tipped back on her forehead to reveal the gently emerging lines there.

She slapped a pudgy hand up to her face. "I don't want to think about it."

"Amanda!" Judy said. "Thirty-three is young!"

"Someone's got a birthday coming up," I said knowingly.

"Don't MENTION it!" Amanda moaned.

Amanda's birthday was September twenty-fourth. The leaves were turning that aged green color that would eventually meld into gold. Amanda worked full-time at the Drummond Island Laundry and Linen Rental, washing and folding sheets and towels for the resorts on the island. She worked hard and came home exhausted. Due to my recent divorce, I hadn't been around much for her. Things were changing for all of us.

"Look at me! I'm forty-two," I said.

"I'm over fifty!" Judy chimed in. "Amanda, you're the youngest of us all!"

"Yep, you're just a puppy," I said.

"Yeah, right." She looked out the window.

Amanda was a hard-core birthday connoisseur. They were important events to her. Not just hers, either. If she knew someone as more than just an acquaintance, she knew when their birthday was. She also could name the year and sometimes even the time of day they had come into the world. Since her thirtieth birthday, I had noticed her having a little harder time with each one. I guessed that was normal.

The weeks passed, and it seemed before I knew it, the end of September was upon us. Of course, I made the trip home to see her with gifts and a card. I sat down at the kitchen table that night with Amanda and asked, "What do you want to do for your birthday tomorrow?"

She had an answer ready. "I want to go up on a bluff and shout out our ages."

I was eating a sandwich, and I paused in midbite. "Really?"

"Yes. You know, up over the houses and people, up high, and shout so everyone can hear."

I nodded. "Okay."

The next day, we drove to the Soo with Judy. We went

to the movies and out to Ang-gio's. We sat in a booth waiting for our pizza and Amanda said, "I put something in your purse, Nancy."

"You did?"

My bag had been sitting in the back seat with her. I unzipped it, dug through it, and pulled out a party favor— a bright pink whistle that unfurled when it was blown into.

"Judy's got one, too," Amanda said.

Judy looked in her purse and, sure enough, she also had a whistle. Amanda reached into her own bag and held up an identical one.

"Wow," I said. "You really plan ahead."

"On three," Amanda said.

We all held the whistles poised to our lips. Amanda held up one finger, then two, then a third. We blew hard, and a loud squealing rose from our table as the whistles unfurled and jostled together. Other diners looked over and smiled.

"Happy birthday, Amanda!" I said.

"Happy birthday! Happy birthday!" Judy agreed.

Amanda beamed. We devoured our pizza and laughed and joked, and then the waitress emerged with a cake and a single lit candle on top.

"Look at this!" I said. I hadn't told them it was her birthday, but someone must have noticed the fuss we were making.

"Isn't that nice of them?" Judy said.

"We have to sing."

Amanda covered her face as Judy and I brayed an off-key version of "Happy Birthday to You" as loud as we could, but I could see that she was smiling.

We left the restaurant, and I drove us up to the campus of Lake Superior State University, where I had attended college years before. Behind the Student Services building, there was an enormous hill that overlooked the International Bridge to Canada. We pulled up alongside some small maples and looked out over the expanse of city far below that was Sault Canada, and the Sault Locks where the big freighters came through. A light breeze blew across the hill from Lake Superior to the west of us.

"This must be the bluff!" Judy said.

"This is it!" We jumped out of the car and walked across the grass, among the young maple trees to the edge of the tremendous steep hill. We were indeed looking down upon the "houses and people."

I turned to Amanda. "Here we are. You have to go first. It's your birthday."

She didn't hesitate. She took a deep breath and roared with all her might. "I'm THIRTY-FOUR! THIRTY-FOUR! I'm THIRTY-FOUR YEARS OLD!"

Judy and I looked at each other, a little startled. We hadn't expected such vocal power from such a little person.

I jumped forward, hopping up and down, and flinging my arms up over my head. "I'm TWENTY-NINE! I'm TWENTY-NINE!"

Judy's voice broke with laughter as she wailed, "I'M TWENTY-SIX!"

"Okay," Amanda said. "I'M TWENTY-FIVE! I'M TWENTY-FIVE!"

"WOO HOO! YEAH!" I yelled, clapping my hands, and we all leaped and cheered, shouting over the rooftops, into the air toward the setting sun.

Nancy J. Bailey

Oh, Happy Day

The other evening, as my little girl was chattering away, she asked me a question that would have seemed inane if posed by an adult. I was busily scrubbing spots out of the carpet (a favorite pastime) when she said, "Mommy, what was the happiest day of your life?" What surprised me was the unhesitant answer that popped out of my mouth: "Aunt Sonia's wedding." My daughter replied, "Really?" I was relieved I didn't hurt her feelings by excluding something like, "Naturally, it was the day you were born, Jordan." Frankly, I don't remember much about that day because I gave birth to twins via C-section, and I was incredibly drugged up. It would have been nice to say it was my own wedding day, but I was too sleep-deprived and anxious to really relax and enjoy it. No, the happiest day of my life was when my family honored my sister on her nuptials.

I've come to enjoy the irony of this epiphany because if asked about Sonia's wedding before it occurred, my reaction would have been different. When she called me twenty-two years ago to announce she'd gotten engaged, I was living in England at the time studying drama. I was quite dramatic when she shared her news. "Oh, Sonia," I squealed, "how wonderful! A wedding, *your* wedding! I can't believe it!" My bubble was about to burst with joy.

Well, she burst it a few weeks later by giving me the wedding date. "The weekend of July fourteenth," she said triumphantly.

"What?" I asked. "July fourteenth? Are you sure?"

"Sure, I'm sure. Why, is there a problem?"

"No, of course not."

I was going to be her maid of honor on July fourteenth—no problem. When I hung up, I felt thoroughly deflated . . . and conflicted. My sister had chosen the only date of the year crucial to me and my narcissism. It was when a small group of American drama-school graduates were to perform a British export in New York and earn their Equity cards. It was the night I was supposed to turn professional and transform myself into a major tour de force.

"Well, of course, you're going to have to miss the wedding," said the director of the school. *Miss the wedding? Bite your British tongue,* I thought. *Miss the wedding? I'm her maid of honor! We're a close family. This is a very big deal.* I might as well have been talking to a bag of fish and chips. The Brits don't make a big splash out of weddings unless, of course, they're royal. "I don't care if it's the deal of the century. It's the weekend of your show, and you can't miss it. If you think you're ever going to succeed in this business, you're going to have to put blinders on and put your career first. Do you understand what I'm saying?"

I understood, but his words stung. "Well," I said, "can you maybe change the date of the play?" Blank stare.

"Well, can you maybe change the date of the wedding?" My sister was horrified. "What, are you serious? Do you know how hard it was for me to get that date? Do you have any idea how many weddings there are in Houston that . . ." Blah, blah, blah. I couldn't push it with her. I was treading on dangerous bridal ground, and she was already getting sensitive. So I pushed it with my mother. "Sweetie, we can't change the date, and you have to be here. Nothing's more important than your sister's wedding." There was no question; she was right. It was settled.

But I was unsettled months later when I returned to the States to prepare for the big event. It didn't help that I had become a pseudosocialist when I was abroad. I walked into a dining room completely adorned with a disgusting, capitalistic display of presents and bows, and I shrieked, "What the heck is this?"

"Oh, some of your sister's gifts. Aren't they pretty?" my mother said. "Now, you go upstairs and shave your underarms and get ready for the Sip 'n See." The what? "Our neighbors are joining us for lemonade and cookies and a viewing of the gifts," Mom said. "Get it? A Sip 'n See."

"How Southern," I muttered, gagging. (Of course, I had my own Sip 'n See five years later.)

But I'd stopped gagging by the time the blessed event occurred. I was floating, and I wasn't even the bride. I was the young, carefree little sister. I will never forget the euphoria I experienced while watching my sister glide down the aisle with both of my parents. She was absolutely stunning. I gazed at her through the night as we all celebrated. My entire family was together—healthy, intact, loving and buoyant. And Sonia was the radiant jewel among the encrusted stones of our gathering. I flashed back to every childhood memory I'd ever treasured: "Sweet Sonia" sharing her ancient Halloween candy with my brother and me. We would sit fascinated as she dumped piece after piece onto the floor. It didn't matter that the candy was over a year old; we were ecstatic. I remembered our ballet classes together. A long-stemmed rose, she at least looked the part of a prima ballerina. I remembered the all-nighters she pulled while still in elementary school. It paid off: Sonia was a chronic straight-A student and a great example to follow.

On that fateful night, I never thought about the New York performance I missed. Today I ponder over it sporadically when I spot a friend on TV. And I still don't have an Academy Award or an impending stroll down the red carpet. But it's like I told the director later, "Without my family, none of it matters." It's a relief to fully respect and appreciate that statement as I mature and raise my own family.

Shelley Segal

READER/CUSTOMER CARE SURVEY

CFEG

First Name		MI.	Last Name

Address			

State	Zip	Email	City

1. Gender
❑ Female ❑ Male

2. Age
❑ 8 or younger
❑ 9-12 ❑ 13-16
❑ 17-20 ❑ 21-30
❑ 31+

3. Did you receive this book as a gift?
❑ Yes ❑ No

4. Annual Household Income
❑ under $25,000
❑ $25,000 - $34,999
❑ $35,000 - $49,999
❑ $50,000 - $74,999
❑ over $75,000

5. What are the ages of the children living in your house?
❑ 0 - 14 ❑ 15+

6. Marital Status
❑ Single ❑ Married
❑ Divorced ❑ Widowed

7. How did you find out about the book?
(please choose one)
❑ Recommendation
❑ Store Display
❑ Online
❑ Catalog/Mailing
❑ Interview/Review

8. Where do you usually buy books?
(please choose one)
❑ Bookstore
❑ Online
❑ Book Club/Mail Order
❑ Price Club (Sam's Club, Costco's, etc.)
❑ Retail Store (Target, Wal-Mart, etc.)

9. What subject do you enjoy reading about the most?
(please choose one)
❑ Parenting/Family
❑ Relationships
❑ Recovery/Addictions
❑ Health/Nutrition
❑ Christianity
❑ Spirituality/Inspiration
❑ Business Self-help
❑ Women's Issues
❑ Sports

10. What attracts you most to a book?
(please choose one)
❑ Title
❑ Cover Design
❑ Author
❑ Content

TAPE IN MIDDLE; DO NOT STAPLE

||| ||

BUSINESS REPLY MAIL

FIRST-CLASS MAIL PERMIT NO 45 DEERFIELD BEACH, FL

POSTAGE WILL BE PAID BY ADDRESSEE

Chicken Soup for the Sister's Soul 2
3201 SW 15th Street
Deerfield Beach, FL 33442-9875

I₁₁II₁₁₁II₁₁I₁₁I₁I₁₁I₁₁II₁I₁I₁₁I₁I₁I₁₁₁I₁I₁I₁₁I₁I₁I

FOLD HERE

Comments

Do you have your own Chicken Soup story
that you would like to send us?
Please submit at: **www.chickensoup.com**

Afternoon Tea

My sister and I always lived near each other, first in New York after we were both married and then in New Jersey, when we both became mothers. We have enjoyed a lifelong closeness and involvement in each other's lives. So when the announcement came thirteen years ago that she and her family were relocating to Arizona, I could not envision living so far apart.

"At least Scottsdale, Arizona, is a place where you would come for a vacation anyway," she blubbered through her tears. When our sobbing subsided, we vowed to do all we could to make our visits meaningful. It was arranged that she and her younger daughter, then age four, would come to New Jersey for two weeks in the summer. I would visit her with my daughter, then nine, over winter break from school at the end of December. This is a pattern that we have continued for all these years.

Each year, as soon as my sister informs me that she has booked her plane tickets to New Jersey, I become a recreation director and delve heartily into the planning for all the exciting things the four of us will do together—Broadway tickets, a hotel stay in New York, museum exhibits, Great Adventure, the Jersey shore. When I book the December flight to Arizona, my sister begins the task of arranging our adventures on her new turf. These adventures have included desert jeep tours; visits to Sedona, Flagstaff and Tucson; the night light show at the Phoenix Zoo; a day at a spa; hiking the mountains in the area; and what has turned out to be the highlight of our visit each year—afternoon tea at the Phoenician Hotel in Scottsdale.

The tea began as an afternoon experiment for just the two of us, as the Phoenician is an elegant hotel and our daughters were too young during the first few years to be trusted amid all that expensive, breakable china. When my niece turned eight and my daughter was thirteen, we decided to include them, and the girls have been eagerly accompanying us ever since. Afternoon tea together for the four of us once a year has become our unique day, our Ladies' Experience.

We begin the day by getting dressed up and made up. No talk of homework or chores. No arguments over television or loud music. Like four giggly roommates in a dorm, we test and share our colorful potions—eye shadow in glittering shades of green and gold, blue and violet. Blushes lusciously named Plum and Rose and Sun-Kissed. We primp at the mirror and critique one another's hairdos and outfits, trying on a pooled assortment of jangling bracelets, sparkling necklaces, and earrings that dangle and tickle our necks. Lost in these trivial decisions, we embrace the lightness of the day, the silliness of our pleasure.

Once we enter the cavernous marble lobby of the Phoenician, we are ready to be escorted to the parlor reserved for the sophisticated pursuit of afternoon tea. We glide after our hostess and slide gracefully onto our plush, upholstered couch. In subdued voices, unusual for us, we discuss the assortment of tea flavors listed in the gold-printed menu. Our favorite is black currant, with its tangy blackberry-like taste.

Sitting erect, ankles crossed demurely, we listen to our server's explanation of the history of the tea-drinking custom, which originated in the Orient, and the description of the designs on the rare pieces of porcelain being used for our tea service. We admire the delicately painted flowers and birds, and nod sagely at the rarity of these patterns. Together, we lose ourselves in the elegance and sophistication of our surroundings, and immerse ourselves in the solemnity of the ceremony of afternoon tea.

When our selections are gently placed before us on the beautifully carved coffee table, we find ourselves eating and drinking in a manner totally unlike our usual. We reach for the little watercress with egg and cucumber with dill cream-cheese sandwiches with care; we taste the scones with utmost refinement of manners, delicately licking our lips and nodding appreciatively at one another as we sample the Devonshire cream topping; we clasp our hands in silent joy as the array of tempting pastries is presented. We ooh and ahh over the tiny custards topped with berries, the mini chocolate mousse pies, the lemon meringue tarts. We watch in awe as the dark tea is poured out of an exotic, painted teapot—a teapot with its own history as part of a partially lost British set—and then we lift our cups to drink with our little pinkies extending outward. We dab at our pursed lips daintily with the soft cloth napkins.

Then we lean back as we imbibe more and more tea and begin recapping our week in Arizona. We tell stories and take some photographs, and laugh and laugh. Then we laugh and laugh some more. Then my sister and I find our minds slipping to the past as we remember tales from our childhood to share with our daughters, providing the girls with material for more laughter, along with information about their mothers.

"Remember the time we . . ." is often greeted with "What?! You did that? No way!" Through our relaxed storytelling, not only do our daughters see that we were young once, but we begin to view our little girls as young women on the road to adulthood. "That must have been nice, the way all the kids in the building played outside together," said my niece one day, musing on our description of the endless sidewalk games of Red Light, Green Light, One Two Three. I looked at her with renewed appreciation.

"That sounds hard," my daughter whispered, listening to us recount the steps involved in carrying food shopping, laundry and our bikes up the four flights of stairs to the family's apartment in our walk-up building. I nodded and squeezed my daughter's hand. The warmth of the tea coursing down our throats mingled with the sweetness of the fruit-filled pastries enhances the meaning of this lovely day.

Every so often, an innocent question makes our teatime more memorable. "A dumbwaiter? What in the world is that?" exclaimed the girls after my sister and I reminisced about our mother's daily communication with our aunt in the apartment upstairs via the building's garbage-collection device. The girls' wide-eyed disbelief catapulted us into gales of hysterical laughter. And when my sister recalled our parents hiding her deceased turtle on the fire escape, she was interrupted with, "Hold on! What's a fire escape?" Fortunately, we were able to refer to the final scene in the film *Pretty Woman* to explain, and all of us felt satisfied that a popular movie could be the vehicle to bridge a generation gap.

On this one outing a year, the four of us are transformed. We are no longer teenagers or middle-aged mothers with the problems and pressures each face. For that afternoon, we are four little girls playing Let's Pretend and Dress Up. We are four rich and poised ladies with not a care in the world. We are four women cementing our bond, reaffirming our sisterhood. Two sisters, two daughters, escaping the mundane concerns of everyday life, escaping the fact that we no longer live in close proximity and have to make do with two trips a year, escaping the passage of time and the intrusion of unpleasantness in life. Through indulging in the fragile magic of afternoon tea together, we allow ourselves to savor, with the tea, the strength and beauty of our bond, which we renew with each visit.

Nothing can replace what my sister and I once had, when our homes were in the same vicinity and our lives more directly intertwined. A quick stop at her house on the way back from the mall, or a message on my answering machine that her daughter is coming over to spend a night—the ease of this kind of contact is no longer possible. But we have dedicated ourselves to remaining close by sharing distinctive experiences in order to make the most of the time together that we do have. The payoff now arrives in the form of our daughters, who seem to feel as close and comfortable with each other as the two of us were as children. So when we say good-bye at the Phoenix airport each year before my daughter and I return to New Jersey, we hug and cry and thank each other for everything. But we also make a promise, a promise that seals the bond of our sisterhood—afternoon tea again next year.

Ruth Rotkowitz

4

OH, BROTHER

A sibling may be the keeper of one's identity, the only person with the keys to one's unfettered, more fundamental self.

Marian Sandmaier

"She's cute, but she's eroding my power base."

Giving Away a Sister

To the outside world we all grow old. But not to brothers and sisters. We know each other as we always were. We know each other's hearts. We share private family jokes. We remember family feuds and secrets, family griefs and joys. We live outside the touch of time.

Clara Ortega

Growing up, there were times when I questioned God's wisdom in creating brothers. My younger brother took great pleasure in teasing and tormenting my sister and me. He stuffed plastic worms in the bathtub faucet so that they would spew forth when I was sent up to take my bath. He read our diaries. He revealed our deepest, darkest secrets to friends and foes. He snuck up behind us and mussed our carefully coifed and sprayed hair. He even showed our naked baby pictures to potential boyfriends. In my eyes and those of my sister, our little brother could be a spoiled, rotten pest! Through the years, my sister and I endured a great deal from our little brother who all too soon grew to be taller than each of us. But while his physical stature may have matured, we both secretly wondered if his emotional maturity would ever match that which we most assuredly possessed. It took many years for us to realize that indeed it had.

When my oldest sister announced that she was getting married, her announcement was met with mixed feelings. While we certainly wanted her to have the happiness and joy associated with marriage, our family was in the midst of a trying time. My father had been diagnosed with multiple sclerosis, a debilitating disease that was taking a toll on his life. The good days were becoming far less frequent and the bad much more common. Many days, Daddy, who should have been in the prime of life—in his mid-forties with three grown, successful children and a beautiful granddaughter—was resigned to hobble around with a cane, if he was able to hobble around at all. We all knew that the possibility of Daddy walking my sister down the aisle was slim.

While each of us silently contemplated the situation at first, as the wedding day approached, a discussion among the family was inevitable. Like so many future brides, my sister envisioned herself in white satin walking down the aisle on her father's arm. But as the MS continued to wreak havoc on Daddy's weakening body, it became evident that, despite all efforts to scale down the ceremony and make it as private an affair as possible, Daddy simply would not have the strength to walk down the aisle with his firstborn child. Furthermore, his pride, which was all he had left, would not permit the use of a wheelchair. Daddy was devastated. My sister was heartbroken.

And that is when I discovered that my little brother had indeed reached maturity. Without hesitation, he announced that he had been trying to give his sisters away for years. He assured us that he knew exactly what to do. So on a cold, blustery February day, my sister, an absolute vision in white satin, walked down the aisle on my tall, handsome brother's arm. He held his head high as he stopped beside my father's chair, standing right beside the seated man whom I suddenly realized he was so much like. When the preacher asked, "Who gives this woman to this man?" my brother quietly turned and helped my father rise and take his daughter's arm. In a proud voice, my father announced, "Her mother and I." A daughter's vision and father's duty were fulfilled.

Daddy passed away less than two years later, succumbing not only to the multiple sclerosis, but cancer as well. Daddy left a very big pair of shoes for my little brother to fill, but my brother had already shown, despite his antics, that they were a good fit. In the years that have passed, he has on many occasions taken on the responsibilities that only a fine and good man could. Daddy would be proud of his boy, my younger brother. I am, too.

As my sister, brother and I enter our forties, there are still times when my brother is every bit the pesky little brother from our youth. At family gatherings, he still insists on mussing my hair. (These days, however, there is less to muss.) He takes immense pleasure in persuading my two children to do the very things that he knows I would never allow, like drinking sodas high in caffeine and eating chocolate before bedtime. He even torments my neurotic dogs. I am, however, still the older and wiser sister. He has three children and a larger, even more neurotic dog. I just get even.

Terri Duncan

Across the Miles

*We cannot all do great things, but we can do
small things with great love.*

Mother Teresa

A phone call across the Atlantic between the United
States and Europe in 1980 cost about five dollars a minute.
There was not much time to say more than a quick
"Happy Birthday" or "I miss you." How could my sister
and I remain close when I lived so far away?

We had lived a grand childhood, my sister and our three
brothers, in an old Victorian parsonage in the center of our
New England town. Ann was the reverend's oldest child,
and through the years, she consoled us, cracked us up and
corrected our English. She also drove me to a Beatles concert, advised me about girls, and even pretended to like
The Three Stooges once in a while. In short, she was always
there. One family photograph shows her lifting me, as a
toddler, up to the mailbox so I could put in a letter. We
believed that we "would always be together, if the fates
allow," as the Christmas song goes. However, the fates
were not quite so kind. Love for a Swiss girl tore me away

from my home and family and brought me to the world of banks and watches and five-dollar-a-minute phone calls. It was a painful choice, and the adjustment was difficult. Yet, through it all, my sister weaved her magic.

Before the days of e-mail, faxes, chat rooms, text messaging and cell phones, she talked to me regularly through the only way possible—long, loving letters and a beautiful greeting card on my birthday. Every day I checked my mailbox for signs of the envelope with the blue and red border and the words *par avion*. We shared everything about love, life and laughter and, most important, expressed our affection for each other. Across the miles, she continued to console, crack up and correct.

Suddenly, the letters stopped. Had I said something wrong? I grew more nervous each day as my mailbox provided no *par avion*. Attempts at phone calls went unanswered. Then, one day, I realized just how strong a sister's love can be. As I was returning from a trip to the grocery store, I was struck utterly speechless as I saw my sister standing at the front door to my apartment building. She had flown from Massachusetts to Zurich to surprise me on my birthday. She handed me a greeting card, saying, "I wanted to deliver this one personally." We embraced in a flood of emotion. That day, a revelation took place: we realized that time and distance would be no match for a sister's love.

That card, now twenty years later, is displayed in my Swiss office. Among the cold office equipment is a warm reminder of what it means to be a sister. Now I hold the card in my hands and read one more time: "Across the miles, my heart is with you always." I smile and whisper, "Annie."

Arthur Bowler

My Treat, Sis!

The heart is where great symphonies are born.

Calvin Miller

The fall after my father died, my mother enrolled me in tap and ballet classes.

Even at age seven, I understood money issues existed within the household, especially since Mom had become a widow and had to get a full-time job.

When this opportunity arose, I could hardly believe it; my wish had come true.

I remember asking how we could afford it.

Mom would smile and say, "We'll just have to watch our pennies."

"I'll treasure this forever," I told her.

Saturday mornings, Mom and I would take the bus up South Orange Avenue to Greta Reilly's School of Dance. Many times, when Mom had to work, my seventeen-year-old brother, Sonny, would have to take me. He never complained—contrary to how teens are supposed to react when having to baby-sit a younger sister. In retrospect, he seemed to enjoy it. I think the responsibility made him feel like an adult.

Sonny didn't just ride the bus with me—a half-hour each way—and sit in the waiting room until my hour lessons ended. No, not him. He'd always sit on a chair in the corner of the dance studio where he could watch the class do their warm-up exercises, learn new dance steps, and practice, practice, practice for the year end's recital. He never said much about the class activities, but he did compliment me and my friends on how well we were doing and how hard we worked.

One day on the trip home, he asked, "What are those little shiny suitcases most of the girls bring to class?"

Now I didn't own one, but I explained they were dance cases that held a change of clothes and the shoes needed for both lessons.

Before he could stop his question, he blurted out, "Why don't you have one?" As a look of gloom covered his face, he quickly added, "Sorry."

I assured him it wasn't a problem. The paper shopping bag with string handles I carried my dance stuff in held everything just fine. Actually, the bag displayed my personal touch—colorful swirls and other eye-catching designs, and I could change the bag anytime I wanted.

"Yeah," he agreed. "It works."

Besides, I appreciated just being able to go to class and have the tap shoes and ballet slippers. I didn't need any of the fancy stuff.

A few weeks after the suitcase conversation, I came home from school to find my trusty paper shopping bag sitting on the kitchen table in a strange, bulging shape. My immediate investigation revealed a black shiny dance case framed with silver studs. I don't know how long I stared at it; I was dumbfounded by its presence.

My trance broke when Sonny said, "Hope you like it."

"Like it? I love it! But where did it come from?"

"My treat, sis."

I gave him a big hug and kissed his cheek. "Thank you so much! It's beautiful!"

His face beamed with satisfaction.

"How did you manage this?"

"I just watched my pennies like Mom does."

His delight came from making me happy; mine came from knowing how special he made me, his little sister, feel.

"I'll treasure it forever," I told him.

He smiled. "I even put your shoes and dance clothes inside. Open it up so you can see how everything fits in there."

Gone were the days of paper shopping bags with string handles.

The shiny black dance case survived for only six years of tap and ballet lessons and dance recitals, but its memory and the feeling of being a special little sister still lives in my heart where I'll treasure it forever.

Helen Colella

A Job Well Done

A brother is a friend given by Nature.

Jean Baptiste Legouve

I would have loved to have been a fly on the wall in that two-bedroom apartment. My daughter, Becky, had moved into an apartment with her twin brothers, Brad and Chad. The boys are almost five years older than Becky.

During their childhood years, Brad and Chad watched closely over their little sister. There wasn't a boy anywhere who would hurt Becky. They knew they would have to answer to her two big brothers if they did.

Brad, Chad and Becky all decided to attend the same university the year Becky graduated from high school. It made sense to us that they could share an apartment. It would save us a great deal of money on housing.

As an added benefit, we knew that Brad and Chad would make sure Becky stayed safe. We also decided that the college-aged men would probably stay clear of the apartment if her brothers lived there with her. This was the perfect housing arrangement as far as we were concerned.

One afternoon shortly after classes began, my telephone rang at work. "Hello," I answered.

I heard a disgusted voice on the other end of the line. "Mama," Becky said, "you have to do something. Brad and Chad are worse than you or Daddy. They won't let me do anything."

"I'll take care of it, Becky," I uttered.

I smiled as I hung up the telephone and felt a strong sense of relief. I knew I didn't have anything to worry about. Brad and Chad were doing their job well.

Nancy B. Gibbs

"My new sister is really smart. She already knows enough to spit out vegetables."

Running Away

The play was a great success, but the audience was a disaster.

Oscar Wilde

"I'm running away from home!" my little brother yelled as he stomped toward the back door.

Scared, I ran to my big sister. She'd know what to do. She was wise. She was resourceful. She was almost in fifth grade.

"Angela!" I called, bursting through our bedroom door. Her long ponytail draped onto the book she was reading, all curled up on her bed. "Mitch is running away from home!"

She dropped *Ramona the Brave*, and her feet hit the floor. Mom only worked three afternoons a week, and we'd convinced her that we did not need a sitter. Angela had taken a baby-sitting class, and I had earned the childcare badge in Girl Scouts. We could take care of ourselves, for heaven's sake. But losing our little brother on the first day would likely unconvince Mom in a hurry.

"I tried everything," I said, trying not to cry. "I told him that we love him, that he had no place to go, that it would be really cold at night. I didn't know what else to say. I thought of everything I could."

We scurried to the back door where we found Mitch just standing there.

"Mitch," Angela began sweetly.

"I'm leaving, and you can't make me stay!"

"Where will you go?" she asked.

I'd already thought of that.

"I don't know yet."

"What will you eat?"

I'd thought of that, too.

He grabbed an apple out of the lunch sack he clutched in his fist and waved it at her. Then he opened the door.

"Wait!" Angela said. "You can't leave yet."

"Why?"

She didn't say anything for a few seconds and then blurted out, "You can't leave until after the talent show!"

Talent show? I hadn't thought of that!

"Yes!" Angela took his hand and led him to the couch. "Have a seat." Then she announced like the ringmaster at the circus, "The show is about to begin!" Grabbing my hand, she dragged me to our bedroom.

Mitch called out, "Okay, but it better be quick 'cuz I'm leaving!"

Angela and I rustled through our closet, jabbering and planning, and within minutes she entered the living room with a shawl around her shoulders and *The Sound of Music* songbook in her hands. The dining room floor next to the living room was six inches higher, providing a perfect stage. I plopped next to Mitch to double her audience size, and she began to sing real high.

"I'll climb every mountain, swim every sea, follow every rainbow, if you please won't leave me."

Mitch rolled his eyes and stood up. I shoved him back

onto the couch and raced to the bedroom. "Wait!"

Minutes later, I stumbled down the hall and into the living room . . . er, performance hall . . . wearing my ballet leotard and tutu. I pliéd and tippy-toed and twirled, waving my arms toward him, then toward me over and over again, then clenching my heart, I finally collapsed at his feet like a wounded swan. Mitch looked more confused than convinced and simply said, "I'll get my coat."

"Wait!" Angela pleaded. "I wrote a poem just for you."

Mitch slumped back onto the sofa and rolled his eyes.

This time she had a beret sitting sideways on her head and a tablet in her hands. In a voice that sounded more like our English teacher, she began.

> Please, please, Mitch, don't run away.
> I need you here so we can play.
> We'll play *Star Wars* in dirt and make a mess.
> I'll never again make you wear a dress.

Before he went to kindergarten a couple of years ago, he'd been a much better sport at our tea parties.

He pushed himself off the couch just as I showed up with my hula hoop around my waist. Angela and I had been practicing a lot, and I was up to six consecutive revolutions, including the four on its way down to my ankles. I swirled my hips as hard as I could while Angela clapped and pretended to be impressed.

Mitch was not.

He headed for the door.

"Okay, then," Angela said, as if she was giving up, "if you're going to leave, we'll help you pack."

Mitch looked confused. Me too.

"You go to your room and get your coat, and we'll get the other stuff you'll need out there on your own."

"Fine, then!" Mitch tromped down the hall to his bedroom.

Angela hurried to ours and got our suitcase from under the bed.

"Ramona had this idea in my book," she whispered. We hustled to the living room and the encyclopedia shelves. There we fit volumes A to M into the suitcase and snapped it shut.

Mitch came back into the room with his coat on, looking sadder than I'd ever seen him.

"Good-bye then," Angela said all happy-like, and she motioned to the suitcase.

"Good-bye," Mitch mumbled, grabbing it.

He tried to lift it, but it wouldn't budge. He grunted, but Aardvark to Mussolini was too heavy for him. Finally, he started to drag the suitcase to the back door. With his hand on the doorknob, he turned and stared at the songbook, the tablet, the tutu, the hula hoop and the pleading look in his sisters' eyes.

He smiled just a little. "Okay, I guess I'll stay. But only until tomorrow."

Christie Rogers
As told to LeAnn Thieman

Little Sisters Always Win!

Family isn't about whose blood you have. It's about who you care about.

Trey Parker and Matt Stone

"Time for dinner, time for dinner, time for dinner!" she ordered while walking all over my jigsaw puzzle. I had worked on the dumb thing for hours, and now my bratty little stepsister was kicking it all over the bedroom.

So I did what any self-respecting big brother would do: I gave her a big, fat charley horse right in the middle of the thigh muscle, where it really counts. Screaming as though I had just drowned all the puppies in the neighborhood, she hobbled toward the kitchen like a civil-war amputee, crying out to her stepfather for justice. I overheard the brief, muffled conversation between her and my dad. Then I felt the house shaking as his thunderous footsteps made contact with the hardwood floor in the hallway.

I sat in the room awaiting my fate. I knew I was dead meat; I was older and a boy. She was younger and a girl, and that combination assured her a speedy and favorable settlement in any dispute between the two of us.

"Did you hit her?" asked my father, standing under the doorjamb wearing his most feared expression.

"She kicked my jigsaw puzzle all over the room!" I pleaded, knowing what would come next.

"DID YOU HIT HER?!" roared the voice of doom. You can probably guess how the rest of the one-sided confrontation progressed.

I first met my stepsister outside of a hotel about three miles from the main lodge at Mammoth Mountain, California. When I think back on it, I imagine it served as a test meeting for both families. She and her two younger brothers stood outside the hotel in the parking lot, bundled up to the chin in ski gear. We fumbled through a series of hellos and then went to the lifts for a day of skiing. As kids usually do, we adapted pretty quickly and soon were pushing each other off couches, fighting for food and slopping it up outside in the snow. We spent quite a few winters at different ski resorts together over the years, having fun and trying our best to get on each other's nerves.

I think she enjoyed having a big brother dropped into her life. Big brothers must be more fun to annoy because she took to it like a natural. In our first years together, she would grab any chance to needle me into a fit of rage, pinching me, taking things without asking or setting me up for a fall in one way or another. I earned my driver's license a few years before she did, so I enjoyed the pleasure of ferrying her and her two brothers around town on a weekly basis. There can't be anything worse than playing taxi to a bunch of screaming junior-high-school girls as you drive by a group of your friends at the beach.

A funny thing happened, though, on the way to adulthood. I left high school just as she entered, and all of a sudden she and her group of friends looked quite different. Now my buddies and I had a constant stream of cute

high-school girls running in and out of the house day and
night. My stepsister became less of a burden and more of
a confidante. As we combined forces to feed each other
dates and advice, we actually grew to become good
friends. However, that didn't stop her from sticking it to
me every once in a while. I remember one night down at
the beach when she and I took a long walk together on the
boardwalk. I talked to her about an important occurrence
in my life, describing the events in great detail. I told her
how important it was to me, and how glad I felt that she
wanted to listen.

"Well, there's something I wanted to talk to you about
as well," she said after I completed my lengthy narrative.
She proceeded to tell me I had a big head and that I really
should come back down to Earth where the rest of the
family lived. Just because I had made progress in a popular sport was no reason to elevate my status to the point
where everyone couldn't stand being around me. Oh, and
of course she was telling me this for my own good because
she loved me.

I looked at her for a long time after she finished telling
me what a jerk I was. I couldn't help thinking about how
far the two of us had come together. From two crazy kids
to a couple of young adults trying to make their mark in
the world, she and I had survived each other pretty well.
All the brief conversations we've had since then surely
reinforce that belief. She's a wife and mother now, and I
have a family of my own. Every once in a while, however,
I reminisce about the crazy times we had growing up
together.

It brings me all the way back to that little bedroom at
the First Street house. I knew my dad would clobber me
for giving her exactly what she deserved, but the only
thing that mattered was letting her have it. It's a source of
twisted pride, even after thirty-five years, and even with

the memory of that voice smashing against my forehead as it echoed around the bedroom.

"Don't ever HIT HER AGAIN!"

If I close my eyes tightly enough, I can still see her standing behind my dad, suddenly straight-legged and without pain, with that hideous little smirk plastered on her face. She had landed me in the hot seat and wanted me to know it. That's what little sisters do, and they're very, very good at it.

Kevin Kilpatrick

"It's a nursery, son, not an orphanage."

Phone Call from God

Love builds bridges where there are none.

R. H. Delaney

"You're having surgery *when*? Okay, I'm marking it on my calendar right now. Tell Don we'll be right there with him in the waiting room."

As dozens of friends and family members called with that same message, I had visions of so many visitors at the hospital they'd have to take numbers to get a seat. *How wonderful to be so loved! How Don would enjoy all their support!*

The week before my scheduled date, I called my surgeon's office to make sure I knew all the instructions I would need to follow.

"Arrive at the Outpatient Pavilion next Wednesday at twelve noon," the nurse said. "You'll have some tests first. The surgery itself is scheduled for 4:15. Nothing to eat or drink after midnight Tuesday night, except for your normal pills. Bring loose clothing to wear. You'll go home that same evening; someone will need to drive you. Got all that?"

"Yes, thanks." Simple enough. In fact, since the hospital

was only half an hour from home, I'd have plenty of time to get there.

Then I received still another phone call. "Bonnie, we heard about your surgery. We'll be at the hospital at three to see you before you go under. Take care."

Yes, a call similar to the others—but different enough to put me in a panic. For this one was from a brother who loved me dearly—but had long held a grudge against my husband. In fact, he had neither seen nor spoken to Don for nearly thirty-seven years, until my mother's funeral the previous spring. *What if he got into an argument with Don in the waiting room and made a big scene in front of all my friends who'd promised to be there?*

I sadly called back my friends. "Uh, look," I stammered, "it might just be better if you didn't come. Thanks, anyway." Then I prayed to God not to let my worst fears happen.

The next Monday at 6:30 P.M., just before leaving the house for a meeting, I got still another call. "This is the hospital," said the crisp voice at the other end. "We want to make sure you have all the instructions for your surgery Wednesday."

So I recited all the directions that I had written down. "Good, good. And do you know what time to check in?"

"Yes, twelve noon."

"At twelve? Oh, no! Who in the world told you that? You need to be here no later than eleven."

That Wednesday, Don and I dutifully arrived at the hospital at eleven and signed in. When the receptionist saw my name, she frowned. "What are you doing here so early, Mrs. Hanson?" she asked. "You're not supposed to be here till one."

"Now wait a minute!" I protested. "Someone from this hospital called Monday evening at 6:30 and told me to be here at eleven this morning."

"Impossible!" she huffed. "The office that makes those calls is never open later than five."

By now I was getting a little testy, too. "But I did get a call. If not from your office, then who called me?"

"I don't know," she answered, "but I'll find out." So while I waited, she contacted several people in her office, then in my surgeon's office, then in my regular physician's office.

Finally, she announced, "Just as I said, Mrs. Hanson, no one called you. It was all your imagination. So you can go back home and return at one o'clock, or just sit here and wait."

"But I *did* get that phone call!" I insisted. Steaming, I returned to my seat. I was full of dread about my brother's coming. I was starving and had to miss lunch. I wasn't looking forward to the surgery and all its pain. I couldn't have been more miserable. And now to be insulted like this!

A few minutes later, a kind nurse said, "Mrs. Hanson, since you're here early, we might as well go ahead anyway and do all your tests." Unfortunately, those tests were extremely painful. But both the nurse and the attending physician were very sympathetic and said they'd be praying for me.

When I finished, another nurse rushed in. "Guess what, dear? The surgery before yours has been canceled. Since you're here and your tests are already done, the doctor can take you at two o'clock instead of 4:15!"

I had already asked my friends not to come. My family, except for Don, wouldn't be here until five, but my brother and his wife were coming at three. So I'd be in surgery when they arrived—and not able to act as a peacemaker between them and Don.

Dear God, I prayed frantically as the anesthetic took hold, *I know you're in the miracle business. We sure could use one right now!*

Well, when I finally came to, I was conscious of laughing voices and smiling faces. Don, my brother and his wife! All standing side by side like old friends, joking and telling stories. Impossible!

I opened my eyes in wonderment. "Since you were in surgery when they got here," Don explained, "we all went out to lunch together."

"And had a great time," they laughed. Then they gave me a toy angel bear, flowers, and lots of hugs and kisses.

And, oh, so much more! For what an amazing thing God had done! If I hadn't gone to the hospital early and thus had my surgery early, they wouldn't have been thrown together for lunch—just the three of them. And, with God's help, erased that barrier of thirty-seven bitter years as if it never existed, giving me back my brother.

Of course, I wouldn't have gone in early if I hadn't received that phone call—the phone call that the hospital insisted "nobody made"—but that God of miracles had planned long before.

Bonnie Compton Hanson

Smart in His Own Way

Nothing splendid has been achieved except by those who dared to believe that something inside them was superior to circumstance.

Bruce Barton

"Why can't you be smart like your sister?" my mother would groan after looking over Ron's dismal report card.

My brother would shoot me a nasty look, as if I had somehow goaded my mother into saying that. I'd squirm and look away, uncomfortable at being thrown in his face like that.

But the differences between us weren't just academic. I was the follow-the-rules, afraid-of-her-own-shadow type, while Ron relished the role of rebel without a cause.

Once he threw a boy named Richard into the school's idle incinerator and locked him in. The poor kid yelled and pounded on the door for an hour before a custodian let him out. Another time when Ron was in training to be an altar boy, he and another boy got into the cabinet where the priest kept the wine for mass. Needless to say, a few bottles later, he and his partner in crime never made it out of the trainee stage.

The most embarrassing moment, at least for me, was a time when the entire student body of St. Leander's Grammar School had lined up in rows after recess. The principal, a hawk-eyed Dominican nun, shrieked, "Ronald Martin, I want to see you right now." My cheeks burned with shame as Ron, grinning like the Cheshire cat, strutted and clowned the whole way up to Sister Laura, who conked him on the head with her handheld school bell for committing his latest infraction. *How could this stupid idiot be related to me?* I wondered. Walking back to his place in line, Ron just soaked up the attention from his buddies who punched him on the arm in loving tribute to his daredevil streak.

Whenever my mother scolded my brother for his rowdiness and poor grades and, to my chagrin, compared him to me, my dad would quietly take his side. He'd slip his arm around Ron's sagging shoulders and give him a gentle pat. "Now, Mary, pipe down," he'd cajole. "Ron's smart in his own way." I would stare at Dad, incredulous at how he could ever see anything even remotely smart about moronic Ron.

It wasn't until he got picked up for joy riding in a car he'd hot-wired that Ron's career as a prankster finally ended. By that time, he'd pretty much decided school was over for him anyway. So he dropped out and joined the navy at age seventeen. He must have taken to the discipline of navy life because when his enlistment was over, he got a job working at the Naval Air Station in Alameda, California, repairing airplanes and helicopters. Eventually, he became an expert in aircraft examination and evaluation, supervising a section that was so hardworking and loyal to him that they won an award for a unique achievement: no one took sick leave for an entire year. They loved working for Ron.

But I didn't really discover his true talents until my mother had to have surgery for colon cancer, and my dad asked us to stay with him during my mother's hospitalization.

I'd always known that Ron was a snorer, but I didn't know to what extent until that first night when the wall between our rooms shook with ungodly sounds like someone was strangling a grizzly bear. I got up and opened his attaché case, which he'd shown me once before, where he kept the ear muffs he used in the repair hangars at work, hoping that they'd deaden the noise enough for me to get some sleep. As I put on the mufflers and adjusted the head band, my eyes wandered to some photos sitting on top of a bunch of papers in the case.

There was Ron shaking hands with a rear admiral in a group of navy dignitaries. Another picture showed him receiving a plaque. Still another had him accepting a $10,000 check, again surrounded by top navy brass. I was stunned. I had no clue why my brother, of all people, would be showered with attention like that. He'd never told us about getting any kind of recognition.

The next morning, I asked him about the photos. Almost like a confession, Ron revealed that he had received countless awards during his career: awards for more efficient airplane and helicopter designs, sustained performance, superior performance, zero defect, group and individual awards, even beneficial suggestion awards given by the government to individuals who provided suggestions that saved money on production.

"Why the secrecy?" I asked. He just shrugged his shoulders and looked off for a bit. Then he turned toward me with a sheepish grin on his face.

"Remember when Mom would get on my case, and Dad would say I was smart in my own way?" he asked.

I nodded.

"Well, I always knew I wasn't book-smart like you, but

it wasn't until the past few years that I figured out what I *was* smart in." He pointed to the attaché case. "Now I know."

I just shook my head in awe and smiled back at him, mutual pride and admiration swelling our hearts for the first time in our lives. At that moment, at long last, we both realized we loved and accepted each other for who we were as individuals.

A few years later, I was teaching curriculum and instruction to student teachers at a local university when Ron developed pancreatic cancer and died. I cried for the little boy who never knew how smart he'd been and for the man who'd had such a short time in life to realize his greatness and take pride in his accomplishments. Although Ron had always been smart, it wasn't until the end of his life that he ever really *felt* smart. This was wrong, and I decided to do something about it.

I had been reading about Gardner's theory of multiple intelligences, which outlined the many ways to measure intelligence. For example, some people are linguistic; others are musical or artistic. Ron's intelligence had shown itself in solving mechanical problems and inventing innovative parts for aircraft.

I found a lesson plan someone had written called "100% Smart" and implemented it with my student teachers. First, we brainstormed all the ways people could be smart. Then the students picked ten items from the list and made a pie chart, showing the percentage of each quality they felt they had in themselves. We assigned colors to each category (i.e., logical-mathematic was blue; body-kinesthetic was green) and after coloring in their charts, the students posted them around the room. Instantly, everyone could see that each individual was 100 percent smart—just in different ways.

I used that lesson plan for the six years I taught at the

university, hoping that my student teachers, in turn, would use it with their own students on the first day of school as an icebreaker and self-esteem builder. Ron's experience had taught me that children should never be made to feel less than smart, even if their grades in school didn't always measure up. They will eventually find their own way—just like my genius brother Ron did.

Jennifer Martin

Pedestal Plates and Paper Doilies

People are motivated more by love and joy than anything else.

Henry H. Mitchell

"So, do you like Teresa after meeting her for the first time?" Denise asked me during an early-morning phone call.

I danced around her question, unsure as to why I was feeling reticent about revealing my answer. "She's a great cook—my brother is going to enjoy that! The oatmeal cake she brought was delicious," I said after a thought-filled pause.

I sensed Denise wanted more information, so I tried a waggish distraction. "She was kind to me by leaving the candles off the cake and not reminding me of yet another birthday." Another long silence over the phone told me my diversion had failed.

In an attempt to recover, I said, "She's nice, and she certainly loves my brother. I've never seen him happier!"

My brother, Randy, who was nearing forty-six years old, was getting married for the first time in May. His fiancée, Teresa, was a lovely woman with three teenage daughters; in every way it seemed Randy had chosen quite suitably. Teresa was friendly and cheerful, her smiles generous and her laughs ready. What more could matter?

As I was putting the dining room back into order, it occurred to me that, yes, something else did matter. What I needed was a meaningful connection with my soon-to-be and first sister-in-law.

The previous day, Teresa had baked an old-fashioned oatmeal cake for my birthday get-together. Its four layers were slathered with rich cream-cheese frosting, and it was invitingly presented on a metal pedestal cake plate with a puff of white paper doilies peeking out from its edges.

As I was tidying up the kitchen, I picked up Teresa's cake plate and carefully removed the cake and doilies onto a utility plate. *Doilies are a nice touch,* I thought, *and it seems I'm not the only one who still feels frilly white paper doilies accent presentations with a cheerful elegance.*

I started to put the pedestal cake plate into the dishwasher, but then I realized the dishwasher was too harsh for the well-worn family treasure. The somber gray serving plate could have been silver plate, pewter or aluminum, and it displayed no historical signature of origin. Any esthetic brilliance it once possessed had long ago been worn away.

But beneath the plate's lackluster exterior, it was vibrant with life marks.

It was alive with shiny gouges, black smudge marks, sticky spots and a few tiny cracks in the stem. The cake plate was a living testament of a countless number of birthday parties; anniversary, baptism and graduation celebrations; and church socials.

I hand washed the plate in hot, soapy water and buffed it dry with an embroidered cotton tea towel. Then I placed it on my antique dining-room table that was draped with a white, hand-crocheted tablecloth. It looked beautiful as it sat beaming with the many lives it had touched.

Feeling my face soften with a knowing smile, I picked up the phone and dialed Denise. "Yes, I like her!" I blurted.

Denise seemed puzzled. "What made you decide so emphatically?"

"Would it make any sense at all if I said a pedestal cake plate and pretty paper doilies had everything to do with it?" I laughed.

Cynthia Briggs

"That prince is in for some real sister-in-law problems."

5

SISTERS BY HEART

The desire to be and have a sister is a primitive and profound one that may have everything or nothing to do with the family a woman is born to. It is a desire to know and be known by someone who shares blood and body, history and dreams.

Elizabeth Fishel

Discovering the Joy of Giving

Friendship is one of the sweetest joys in life.

Charles Spurgeon

I was eleven when my grandparents and I fled our Soviet-occupied country, Hungary, into neighboring Austria, with our only worldly possessions—the clothes on our backs. Soon we were transported to a displaced-persons camp, where we joined hundreds of other refugees. The year was 1947.

Our new home, D. P. Camp Spittal, was a self-contained world of barracks lined up like soldiers as far as the eye could see. Although the camp was cramped and dismal, it was an improvement over the life we had known in our war-torn country over the past six years. We had a roof over our heads, we were fed daily, and we were clothed from donations of clothing that arrived regularly from the United States and other countries.

Since most of us in the camp had no money to speak of, we especially looked forward to the distribution of clothes, which usually took place in the spring and in the fall. And if the clothes came from America, we fingered them in awe, for that's where most of us hoped to immigrate.

Of course, the clothes were not new, but they were clean, and we were grateful to get them. Because we were equal in our hand-me-downs, no one outshone anyone else in the camp—until that fall of 1950, that is, when providence allowed me, a teenage refugee girl resigned to not having anything nice, to shine for a while.

We were lined up at the distribution center as usual for our winter garments. The person in charge appeared with an announcement: "This year, a rich lady in America donated something rare to the refugee effort: a beautiful, multicolored fur coat in a young girl's size." He held up the coat so everyone could see it. "Oohs" and "aahs" could be heard throughout the crowd.

"Since we have only one coat and many young girls, we've decided to have a drawing for it. Girls can come up and try on the coat, and if it fits they will write their name on a piece of paper and drop it into this box. Then we will draw the name of one lucky recipient."

"That coat looks like it will fit you perfectly," said my grandmother, who was standing next to me in the crowd. "Go try it on and put your name in the box." I walked up and did just that. The coat was soft and plush and beautiful, and my heart ached to own it. Of course, every girl there felt the same way.

Finally, after a long wait, a small girl reached into the box and drew a name.

"Renie Szilak," the man in charge shouted, waving a piece of paper in the air. "Come up here, young lady, and get your coat."

I stood there in a daze, not quite believing it was true until Grandma nudged me. I finally walked up, feeling hundreds of eyes watching me. When I walked back wearing the coat, I heard a voice in the crowd call out, "You look just like a real princess now!" It was Tibor's voice, the cutest boy in our school. I blushed, but I hoped I was walking regally, as a real princess would.

"I can't believe some girl in America gave up this coat," I said to my friend Piri on our way back to the barracks.

"Maybe it no longer fit her," Piri said.

"But it's so beautiful. I won't give it up even after it no longer fits. It will be mine forever," I vowed.

Piri, who was two years younger than I, had become the closest thing to a sister I would ever have. We lived in the same barrack, and because her father was ill and needed her mother at his side, she spent most of her time with me and my family. Since we had all applied for immigration to the United States, most of our time together was spent dreaming about our future lives in our new country.

The winter of 1950–51 was memorable for me. I turned fourteen, and whenever I wore my beautiful fur coat, I felt like a princess. When I walked to school, the boys who usually ambushed the girls with snowballs let me walk by untouched. And whether the other girls envied or admired me, I knew they couldn't take their eyes off me.

Eventually, spring arrived, and I reluctantly put my precious coat in a box and stored it under my sleeping cot. I hated to put it away, but at least I knew it would be there for me the following winter.

A short time later, our family received the news we'd been waiting for. Our papers were approved, and in September we would board a ship that would take us to our new country, the United States of America! I hurried out to tell Piri the great news, assuming their papers had come through as well. I found her outside the barrack, her eyes red from crying.

"What's the matter?" I asked, sensing what was coming.

"We haven't been approved. They say Papa has TB. Only healthy people can go to America," she replied quietly, instantly turning my world upside-down. We spent the few remaining months glued to each other, but inevitably, the day we had to part arrived too quickly.

On August 1, 1951, Piri and I prepared to say our last farewell before I boarded the transport truck already filling up with departing refugees. The truck was to take us to Salzburg, where our vaccinations would be updated before we'd continue on to the Port of Bremen, Germany, to board the ship taking us to our new country.

"Don't forget me. Write to me," Piri said, holding on to me while tears rolled down her pale cheeks. Her mother, standing next to her, was crying, too. That's when the realization really hit me. We would never see each other again, and they were being left behind while we were starting a new life in a wonderful new country. I realized that instant that I had to do something to try and ease my "little sister's" pain. I broke away and ran after Grandfather, who was boarding the truck with a large box in his hand. I yanked the box away without an explanation and raced back to Piri's side.

"I want you to have the coat, and I want you to know that I will never, ever forget you. How can I forget the little sister that I love?" I said, shoving the box into her hands.

"But . . . you said you would never give up the coat," Piri stammered.

"I'm not giving it up. I'm passing it on to my little sister," I said, tears welling up in my eyes. Then I ran to climb aboard the truck, which was about to drive away.

I will never forget the expression on Piri's face as she stood there teary-eyed, clutching the box, teetering between sadness and glee. It was the moment that I, a mostly selfish fourteen-year-old, discovered the joy of giving. I knew that the gift of a coat was trivial compared to the gift of liberty, but at the time it was the only thing I had to give.

It was mid-November by the time we had a permanent address I could send to Piri. I received her joyous reply a few days before Christmas 1951, and she also enclosed a photo. It showed a girl with long, curly black hair and a beaming smile. She wore a beautiful, multi-colored fur coat, and she looked just like a real princess in it. And that made my heart glad.

Renie (Szilak) Burghardt

A Bona Fide Sister

Between sisters, often, the child's cry never dies down. "Never leave me," it says. "Do not abandon me."

Louise Bernikow

I don't have a sister; I've always wanted one. I'm surrounded by family and friends who have sisters they treasure. Even though my mother and I share a close bond, it's not the same. I see sisters talking with that certain gleam in their eyes, more than the closest relationship with a best friend. I went through life satisfied that I had many close friends that were like my sisters, but I knew the relationships could never have that special bond that they shared with their own female siblings.

I have a friend who said, "The real test of a sisterly bond would be to give up a kidney to save the other's life."

I know I would give up a kidney to save any of my friends, so there has to be something more. Staying the course through a grave illness, I believe, is the real test of having a bona fide sister. It would be easy to give a kidney to someone you loved, but what about the fallout afterward—going through the possible rejection, the renal failure, the heartbreak, the dialysis, the loss? Would the donor still be there, staying the course, to meet the needs of her sick sister? My friend, Linda, did just that when she found out I had ovarian cancer. She was right there, by my side, the day before and the day after my operation.

A few weeks prior to my cancer diagnosis, I was in heart failure. I was told that I had cardiomyopathy, an enlarged heart muscle. I was weak when I started chemotherapy. The day I came home from the hospital, and every day thereafter, Linda came delivering a complete meal for my entire family. I cried; she held my hand. I complained; she listened. When I could barely walk, she was literally and figuratively my support. She came delivering a smile and a reassurance that got me through every rough day, even when the regimen of chemo and drugs affected my mental stability. I didn't want to live. She told me that this feeling would pass, and anytime, day or night, I could call her and she would come to be with me. It wasn't as if she didn't have anything better to do. Linda had health issues with her own family, especially her sick parents.

After nine months of treatment, I was completely bald and had lost over fifty pounds. I looked like a sick bird, but I was finally starting to flap my wings and notice the blue sky waiting for me to fly. Linda gave me more than her time and concern; she gave me the strength and spirit for life, simply by staying the course. She knew I could soar once again; she made me believe it, believing in my ability to heal, not only my body, but my spirit as well.

Family and friends were there for me, but I finally had a true sister, defined by her loyalty. It states, in the dictionary, that a sister is a girl or woman who shares a common ancestry, allegiance, character, or purpose with another or others. By definition, Linda is my bona fide sister; she shares my soul and a reason for living. She will be a part of my heart and fortitude for as long as I breathe. She didn't give me a kidney; she gave me a new mind-set, a new dimension of being that makes me whole, and that certain gleam in my eyes, whenever I share a treasured moment with her.

Dolores Kozielski

Wish Upon a Star

Star light, star bright,
first star I see tonight,
I wish I may,
I wish I might
have this wish
I wish tonight
I wish . . .

I repeated the childhood poem on myriad starlit nights and finished with: "I wish for a baby sister." God would hear, I told myself, for wasn't a wish like mine the same as a prayer? Perhaps God heard, but he chose to answer in a slightly different manner. When I neared four, he sent me a baby brother. At age eight, another brother joined our household. Even so, I continued to watch for the first star of the evening and repeated my wish. No baby sister arrived. When I'd nearly given up, my parents informed me there was to be another baby.

My heart soared with hope. Finally, my baby sister would be a reality. Did it matter that I would be sixteen when she made her appearance? Most assuredly not. All through the months of waiting, I watched for the first evening star and repeated the same words, "I wish for a baby sister." She'd make her appearance in May, which pleased me for it was also my birth month. In May, trees blossomed and grass showed a new spring-green coat, the sun warmed us, and gentle rains urged tulips from their winter's sleep. What more perfect time for my longtime wish to come true?

Dad called from the hospital to tell me that our new brother had arrived. Brother? My heart nearly broke. Three strikes and you're out—baseball or baby sisters, same difference. As disappointed as I'd been, I soon adored my third brother. I accepted the fact that I'd never have a sister. I even stopped repeating my wish whenever I spied the first evening star.

I loved my three brothers, but something seemed to be missing in my otherwise full life.

Girlfriends held special places in my heart throughout high school, college and the newlywed years. I collected friends wherever we lived, but I still felt incomplete in some way. When I heard other women mention their sisters, a little pang rose within me. It couldn't be called jealousy. No, it was more a pang of envy. I chastised myself for feeling this way when I had a wonderful daughter and, as time went on, three beautiful granddaughters.

Once my children were independent, I pursued a life-long wish to write. Many of my stories found a home at an inspirational e-zine. Fan mail arrived from readers, and I soon recognized names of others who wrote regularly for the same site. One in particular wrote often to comment on my stories. It was a mutual admiration society as I loved the folksy humor she injected in each of her stories, the way she taught life's lessons with amazing tales, and the manner in which she used words and phrases. Numerous pictures of her appeared in the e-zine, and I admired the sparkle in her eye and the broad smile in each photo. Our e-mails became more frequent. She lived on a mountaintop, raising donkeys and loving her family. I lived in a university town with neighbors nearby and no pets, but also loving my family. Kathe often mentioned another writer who was also a marvelous editor. Before long, the three of us were good buddies.

In time, our three-way friendship grew strong. In an e-mail, Kathe said she had something serious to discuss, something for me to ponder. Would I consider being her sister since she'd never had one? I knew this was no joke, and I sat in front of my computer feeling stunned. A lump rose in my throat, and tears threatened. Pleasure warmed me from head to toe as my childhood wish was granted in my sixth decade of life. But this would be no baby sister because Kathe was seven years older than me. After all the years of waiting, I wasn't about to quibble. My fingers flew over the keyboard as I wrote a glowing acceptance of her offer to be my sister.

Not long after, she wrote to ask what I'd think about asking sweet Maria to be our younger sister. And so it came to be that we three are sisters of the heart. Kathe is the eldest, I am the middle sister, and Maria is our baby sister. Is it only coincidence that she is the same age as my youngest brother? The messages fly between us. We edit one another's stories before they are sent to an editor. We rejoice when they sell, and we commiserate when they don't. We bare our souls to one another.

This past summer I had the great good fortune to finally meet my older sister in the flesh, since my husband and I would be traveling through her state. I hesitated to suggest a visit, since Kathe had lost her husband only weeks earlier. She immediately told us to come. The long hug we gave one another sealed our sisterly bond forever. We talked nonstop for two days—the way sisters do. Late on the second afternoon, a phone call from our baby sister, Maria, brought more laughs and chatter between the three of us. How wonderful if Maria might have joined us on top of Kathe's mountain.

One day, perhaps, we three sisters of the heart will find ourselves together in a place where we can give hugs whenever we like. Meanwhile, the messages fly through cyberspace. Each one is filled with the love only a sister can pass along to another sister. Now, when I see the first evening star, I repeat the little poem to myself and just smile. My sisters were worth the wait.

Nancy Kopp

Sunshine Sisters

Robbing life of friendship is like robbing the world of the sun.

Cicero

Once in a very great while, along come friends who take a rainbow brush to your black–and–white little life, illuminating possibilities you never fathomed. These lovely ladies make the mundane miraculous, the boring brilliant, and the nothing special anything but. They look past your faults and fears and see a dynamic version of you that you hope truly does exist somewhere deep within. But most of all, they bring the most outrageous adventures across your path and often drag you along.

One of my sunshine sisters is named Dawn, which suits her just fine, for life seems to awaken at her arrival. Interestingly, she is totally unaware of her effect on those around her. I believe she just thinks that is how the world really is, not realizing that things and people are a bit duller without the light she brings.

We met in training to be flight attendants, and we were both sent to Salt Lake City where we shared an apartment. I was relaxing on my day off when she popped through the door still in uniform.

"You off?"

"Yes," I answered tentatively, knowing the question was loaded with possibilities that would probably stretch my comfort zone.

"Great! Let's go camping."

"Where?"

"We'll figure that out as we go."

Knowing that details were never her strong suit and that they truly did not seem to matter in her world, I threw some clothes and gear in a pack, loaded the car, and we were off to . . . well, somewhere.

Eventually, we arrived at Canyon Lands in southern Utah where we registered with the park ranger and got a briefing on primitive camping. "Stay on the trail so as not to disturb the microenvironments that sustain life . . . blah, blah, blah . . . pack out what you pack in, and you must be a half-mile off the trail to make camp." We placed a placard in our car with our return date so they would come looking for us if the car was still there and we were not.

As I placed the blue card on my rearview mirror, pictures of my mom and dad fingering the last tangible thing I touched before "the accident" flashed through my overdramatic mind. We hoisted on our packs, grabbed the trail map and began the hike into the vast open space of red rock. Being a Southerner, I was accustomed to trails marked with paint or flags or etching on trees, or at the very least a well-worn footpath that you could easily distinguish from the natural surroundings. Utah is funny in that the trails are marked every half-mile or so with a stack of rocks that uncannily resembles many other naturally formed stacks of rocks with no discernible footpath connecting them. This did not seem to deter Dawn, nor did the lack of compass, for that matter. I prayed silently, hoped for the best and allowed myself to be distracted with the name game, which Dawn had begun.

Over the next couple of hours, our game was repeatedly interrupted with discussions of stacks versus natural rock formations. At least we could tell which direction was west, since the sun was descending quite rapidly. We reached the edge of the canyon and began slicing switchbacks back and forth across the face, sloping steeply to the unseen bottom. Being a rules follower, as the light seemed to diminish, my anxiety did just the opposite for we could definitely not adhere to rule #3 of primitive camping etiquette: Thou shalt be a half-mile off the trail to make camp. The closest suitable alternative given the conditions was a large, flat boulder five feet off the trail. We pitched the tent in the dark and crawled in, laughing about our adventures thus far and fell into a well-deserved slumber. A resounding CRACK startled us both from our dreams. We found ourselves staring at each other in the perfect light of day, which was a bit disconcerting since it was the middle of the night. Then it was pitch black again. The rat-tat-tat of the raindrops on the outside of the tent helped to disperse the fog of my too-tired synapses.

A thunderstorm.

"Wow! Did you hear that?"

"Heard it, saw it, even kinda felt it!" she chuckled. Taking a cue from her, I began to laugh, and we joked about being washed into the canyon and found it a "good thing" that we had left the blue card in the car so they could find us . . . some day. The rain, thunder and lightning continued, and we felt a small stream had formed, winding its way between the tent floor and the red rock. My laughter began to diminish, and my prayers became more fervent. At some point my fear gave way to exhaustion, for I awakened the next morning to find every muscle in my body aching from being tensed for most of the night. I heard my friend's voice from outside our tent, "You gotta see this!"

I untangled my limbs from my sleeping bag and crawled out of the tiny opening. The morning sun had just begun its ascent, and from our vantage point several hundred feet from the bottom of the canyon, we were in optimum position for its performance. The orchestra of colors synchronized beautifully to the unseen conductor's hand. Each hue harmonized with increasing and decreasing intensity, fulfilling its part in the magical ensemble. There was no need for words; just solemn silence as we absorbed all that was around us. I saw a radiance in her face, and I knew that part of it was saying, "See! Trust me. That sense of lostness, the unknown, yes, even the rain and lightning are all part of it. And without all of it, we would have missed this." I know for a fact that without her urging, I would have missed out on some absolutely amazing moments. It is friends such as these—sunshine sisters—who nudge us out of our comfort zones into the truly magical aspects of life.

Libby Hempen

I Do Have Sisters

One loyal friend is worth ten thousand relatives.

Euripides

I have lived without a biological sister for seventy years, but do not feel sorry for me. I have acquired sisters along the way—loyal women who have shared my interests and passions, good moments and desperate ones. Oh, yes, I do have sisters.

There is Ferida. She shares my writing soul as well as many other parts of me. We can sit for hours, she eating her health food, me devouring as many sugar products as possible, breathing together, almost as one, as we create a story or chase an idea. We weep together when life bruises us. And then there are times we run down the boardwalk as if we are fifteen once more, giggling loudly, waving our hands, acting outrageous as one can do effortlessly with a sister. Ferida never forgets my existence.

And there is Carol. I met her at the darkest time in my life—after cancer and widowhood. We met at a support group. I did not want to be there. We were both in pain, vulnerable and without hope. She picked me up—a broken bag of bones and spirit—and helped me function again as only a sister would. And now, years later, the sisterhood continues, neither one of us letting the other be without hope again.

I include Linda in my circle of sisters as she has been with me through children growing and leaving, and through life changes neither of us expected. Our minds always find a place to meet, though we might not physically be able to do so. Linda does not let me get complacent about anything in life that could be made better. She is so much that I am not. Yet she always makes me feel like so much more. And with her in my life, I am.

They are my sisters. When I am with them, I need not hide my weaknesses nor be anything other than what I dare to be. Oh, yes, I do have sisters. As women, don't we all?

Harriet May Savitz

Surprise Sister

"You need to meet Karin." My friend Sandra was emphatic, as if I had no choice in the matter. "She could be your sister."

"Sure." I was only vaguely interested. Sandra, though a dear, was nearly opposite of me in every way. It was hard to believe she'd know what sort of people I would be attracted to. Besides, I already had several good girlfriends, longtime friends I had grown up with. Then there were my mother and younger sister. I was close to them, too. Friends took time and energy, both of which were in short supply. What could a new friend give me that I didn't already have? But Sandra persisted.

"I'm telling you, Cathy, you two are just alike. Why don't you come to my Christmas party? Karin will be there."

"All right, all right." Sandra was a fun person. It was bound to be a good time, whether this Karin was interesting or not.

Two weeks before Christmas, I pulled up to Sandra's festively decorated home. People milled around the house and spilled out on the deck. I was friendly, but kept to myself. Her friends weren't usually my type.

Then I saw Karin sitting quietly by herself at the back of the room. I knew it was her, even before Sandra enthusiastically grabbed me by the arm and dragged me over for an introduction.

"Cathy, Karin; Karin, Cathy." She smiled with satisfaction, as if a duty had finally been fulfilled, and walked away.

"Hi," I said stiffly. We looked each other over. Sandra was right; there was an uncanny resemblance.

Most of my girlfriends are small and cute while I am unusually tall for a woman. I've gotten used to feeling like an oddity, head and shoulders above all my friends. But Karin was tall, too, fine-boned and slender, just like me. We both had blonde hair that framed a narrow, reserved-looking face. I sat down beside her and tentatively began a conversation.

We uncovered many similarities that night and throughout the beginning of our friendship. Karin has two brothers and a younger sister, just like me. Though she is eight years older, we each have two children: an older boy and a younger girl. Both of us love horses and, when we met, were training a young horse for the first time in our lives. We each prefer outdoor activities, have a tendency to be cheap, rarely watch television and are avid readers. Though we would never buy it, we secretly enjoy *People* magazine. We also live only a few miles apart. It wasn't long before her house and family felt almost as familiar as mine.

Although Karin quickly became a good friend, it took me awhile to realize our relationship was special. About a year after we met, I began hearing strange comments from the people who knew us. They seemed to notice our similarities, too.

"I saw your sister in town," a neighbor informed me one day.

"My sister doesn't live nearby," I said, puzzled.

"Well, she looked just like you."

And the observations kept coming. Soon, it became a kind of joke we enjoyed being part of.

At a horse show one day, a friend of Karin's approached. She looked me up and down.

"Is this your sister?"

"No, we're not related." Karin elbowed me, and I giggled. Somehow we had become sisters, without even realizing it.

Besides our sisterly appearance, Karin does all the things a sister should do. She is always available to share a meal, her clothes, a ride to town, or a glass of wine and a long talk by the fire on a chilly night. We ride our horses, shop for groceries and get massages together. We call with important questions like—"What are you doing?" We are comfortable in silence.

At her house one evening, my husband entered the family room where Karin and I lounged by the fire, reading material in hand.

"I can't believe you two have been sitting here quietly for the whole evening!" He shook his head in disbelief. I just looked at Karin and shrugged. There was nothing to say, only peace in our silent companionship.

When I think about it now, I can hardly remember when Karin hasn't been part of the fabric of my life. Though God gave me a precious biological sister, Karin is the sister my heart chose for itself.

And the question still comes.

"I saw your sister yesterday," an acquaintance informed me recently. "She is your sister, isn't she?"

This time I nod and smile. "Yes, yes, she is."

Catherine Madera

Reprinted by permission of Patrick Hardin ©1987.

Roomies

We were off for a nice, peaceful ride through the island interior—or so we thought. Perhaps we should have been alerted to the possibility of danger when we boarded the tourist bus and found it pulled by a large semi-tractor trailer cab. Perhaps we should have noticed the paper warnings carefully placed on each seat. We discovered later that pregnant women, those with back or heart trouble, the elderly, and those suffering from fear of heights were advised not to ride in this vehicle. But my girlfriend of forty-five years and I were oblivious to everything except each other's company.

When we were seventeen years old, we had met at Brown University as freshmen. We had walked slowly out of French 101 class laughing and talking, not in any hurry to say "so long" at our separate dorms. Every Monday, Wednesday and Friday, I jumped out of bed because those were French class days with Elaine.

College summers at our distant homes gave us an opportunity for a running correspondence. When a typical six-page letter arrived in my mailbox in Elaine's sloping scrawl, I savored every word, then penned an answer as fast as the ink would flow.

Although we were best buddies throughout college, there never seemed to be an opportunity for us to room together. That is until senior year, when Elaine's roommate was recovering from an illness and desired my single room. She asked if I would like to room with Elaine.

"Boy, would I!" I exclaimed.

At last, we were together. We called ourselves "roomies," which in our mind was a synonym for sisters. We shared the same sweaters and skirts, which piled up on a common chair in the center of the room. We met for all three dorm meals—our favorite dish being breaded veal cutlet with tomato sauce and spaghetti.

College hill we traversed arm-in-arm, usually doubled up in laughter. College pressures we vented with our preferred expression, "What a revolting development"—and more laughs, of course.

Even brushing teeth before bed was a social time. When our necks were fully extended to keep the saliva mixed with toothpaste from dribbling out as we talked, we knew the moment had come to visit the sink in the corner of our room. After all, roomies didn't miss a beat of conversation.

With companionship like that, college was ever so sweet.

Rudely catapulted by graduation into the real world, we wondered if distance would keep us from seeing each other again, but it didn't. Elaine came from the East to Chicago for my wedding, and later I journeyed to New York City to meet her and her husband. Again, we met when she was an inner-city social worker, and I was a Peace Corps worker assigned to Africa. We met when she worked on her Ph.D., and I practiced physical therapy along with single motherhood. Likewise, when we both married a second time. And also when she became a published tenured professor in social work, and I an author and Christian speaker.

Even as our ages rose over sixty, we still met—and, of course, laughed like girls, not like Elaine the responsible university dean or Margie the trained foreign missionary. Perhaps our worldviews had taken us in different directions, but who would ever care? We preferred only to celebrate each other's company.

And so it was as we seated ourselves in the front seat of the large bus carriage for the best possible view of the island. The driver put the cab in gear and started up the hill. All was fine as long as the road remained paved. I became suspicious when it narrowed into a dirt track, only slightly wider than a walking path, and the hillside rose into a mountain.

"Are you sure we got on the right tour?" I asked.

"So much for our peaceful valley ride," said Elaine, starting to laugh.

"Look at that drop-off," I said, peering down. "And I'm afraid of heights."

"No worries. Someone put up a little white picket fence to protect us. See?"

"How reassuring," I said as laughter began to put some color back into my blanched cheeks.

Wham. Down we went. "That pothole was more like a sinkhole."

"Rock hard, too. Ouch." My teeth clanked, my brains rattled, and my vertebrae slammed into each other. The softer parts of my body jiggled like jelly slopping out of a bowl.

"There is not a single shock absorber in this bus," I lamented. To get off the hard metal seat, I braced myself on its edge in a half-squatting position.

Just then the cab rounded a hairpin curve, and the shoulder of the carriage where Elaine and I sat was thrust out and over—eek—eternity.

Together we leaned in the opposite direction as if our

hundred-plus-pound bodies could counterbalance the multi-ton bus.

In an instant I was thrown back against her, then tossed up and down and almost on the floor. The relentless jostling persuaded us to abandon futile attempts at self-protection. Instead, we laughed until our sides hurt more than our assaulted body parts.

An hour later in the center of the island, we limped arm-in-arm off the bus to the gift shop—where we remained hopelessly stuck in our laughing jag. People stared at us as we bantered hysterical quips back and forth. Because we looked—and obviously acted—younger than our years, onlookers probably thought we were gals off on a binge. Elaine's husband, a distinguished labor judge, walked a safe distance behind—as if he didn't know us.

"What was so funny on that bus?" he asked later. "How could you laugh when you were in such pain?"

We couldn't even explain it. We just had a way of sparking each other into joy. Proverbs says, "A cheerful heart is good medicine." Roomies know a lot about that, and I am glad Elaine is my roomie for life.

Margaret Lang

Sisters in Our Hearts

When you are with a friend, your heart has come home.

Emily Farrar

I was an only child who liked it that way. Selfish or fool-ish? When asked if I wouldn't like a sister or brother, I told them what my parents had told me, "We got our perfect girl the first time around." I thought that we were happy that way. Then, I married Bill.

He had two sisters who are opposites. One gave mean-ing to the term "sibling rivalry." If there was trouble to be made, she thrived on it. The other was the homemaker par excellence. She canned from her garden, baked bread, made homemade ice cream and could change a tire. We lived a half-day's ride from both of them. That was fine by me. Until . . .

Too late, Bill discovered that he had colon cancer. Joyce went into debt to buy a new car and began visiting us at least a weekend each month. With two teenagers and a job added to my responsibilities, I began to welcome her visits.

One Saturday, when the younger generation had

departed for places well known, Bill called us to his bed-side. As his control over his body ebbed, he began to assert his control in other ways. He outlined his funeral arrangements. Papers here, clothing there, minister and music preferred. He wanted to return to Pennsylvania, which had always remained his home. And then he continued:

"I leave you both the greatest gift of all."

We looked at each other in surprise. What could he mean?

"I leave you each a sister who knows how to be kind, loyal and loving. For yourselves and for me, take care of one another."

Neither Joyce nor I could ever deny him anything, so we clasped hands and promised.

Through taking Bill home from New Jersey to his memorial service for his coworkers and clients who needed this opportunity to give him praise, we walked side by side. Through thirteen years, we've continued our trail of togetherness. Vacations, graduations, hardships and plenty, my sister and I have shared it all.

Bill blessed me with two children. He brought together the resources, spiritual and financial, to give them the wings to soar. But, most of all, he gifted me with a sister. We loved him then, and as life's journey leads us through the lush valley and up the Rocky Mountains, we've learned to love him more. Although he was taken away, he made sure we would never be alone.

Lois Wencil

Fridays

As the pressures of life intensify, sometimes the difference between going after a dream and remaining passive is having someone say, "I believe in you!"

Gary Smalley

"Corn chowder next week," Angela said. "I've got a new recipe."

"I'll bring the wine," Paula said.

"I've got dessert covered," Suzie added. "Brownies and ice cream. What a feast we'll have!"

As always, they arrive Friday at 5:30—Suzie in her cozy sweatpants and Paula adorned with a purse that is bigger than she is. They shed their many burdens at the door and bounce into the kitchen, carrying with them the crisp outside air and their share of the meal. I open the wine to let it breathe while Paula puts on some light music. Suzie cuts up the crusty French bread, and Angela ladles the steaming soup into the bowls.

The rich smell of bacon fills the kitchen. I propose a toast, "To life's celebration!" We hold our glasses together,

wait for the sound of chimes and drink the wine of acceptance. This ritual is the necessary shower that washes off
the stains of life.

But none of us thinks of all that as we enthusiastically
partake of good food. At times, the whole evening is a
burst of laughter if Angela decides to be a comedian. Some
nights are for prayer when one of us is faced with an
insurmountable obstacle. There was Paula's mom's heart
surgery, and Suzie's daughter's nasty divorce; we had a
special dessert the day it was final. And the Fridays roll by,
one by one, steadily weaving threads of themselves into
our lives, into the fabric of time.

Suzie brings the champagne on the first Friday of
January, and we take turns sharing our goals and dreams,
toasting the New Year's many promises. Then we each
live our lives as the months unfold before us—filled with
painful challenges and delightful surprises—but Friday
always comes around.

Salads replace the heavy soups, brownies turn into
strawberry shortcakes, and the dinners are moved to the
patio. We put sweaters on and take in the wet smell of
spring dirt. The tulips' first buds emerge, then an explo-
sion of color. Before long we see them fade to nothing,
lazily recessing into the ground until the next spring.
Sweaters are shed, and we eagerly wait for the birds to
grace us with their evening songs as we talk and laugh. We
light vanilla-scented candles and watch God's rainbow of
color while the sun lowers in the summer sky. Our birds
take off at the first signs of cold, and the dinners are
brought inside, the fireplace warming us on cool fall
evenings. And then the heavy coats come back, and the
boots are covered with snow. Cinnamon is in the air.

And the Fridays march on. The four old friends are getting older. The four old friends are turning into sisters.

"I'll barbecue pork chops next week," Angela said.

"Marinated with garlic and balsamic vinegar."

"I've got the perfect wine for that!" Paula said.

"I'll make a salad," I said.

"And I'll bake us some fancy-schmancy peach pie," Suzie added. "What a feast we'll have!"

Barbara A. Croce

"Okay, I'll tell you, but this has to stay
locked in the Sister Vault."

The Promise

Sometimes our light goes out, but is blown into flame by an encounter with another human being.

Albert Schweitzer

Potluck roommates, that's how we met. Solo travelers joined together for a two-week tour of Israel and Egypt. At first glance, we didn't seem to match at all. Kelly's not quite five feet tall, with curly blonde hair and bright blue eyes. And I'm a svelte five feet, eight inches tall, with straight dark hair and serious black eyes. We may have looked like total opposites, but soon after saying hello, we discovered we had kindred hearts.

Kelly and I shared a passion for travel. This trip to the Holy Land was just what we needed, each for very different reasons. At thirty-nine, Kelly was five months' pregnant. She traveled alone because her husband stayed behind to run the Western wear company they owned. Conversely, I traveled alone because my marriage had ended five months earlier.

For Kelly, this trip to the Holy Land was a pilgrimage.

She hoped to prepare herself for the gifts and challenges that would accompany motherhood.

My dream of being a wife and mother had recently been shattered by divorce. I went to Israel desperately searching for hope.

The first time we sat down for a meal, Kelly and I knew we were kin. Scooting into the booth, I ordered a grilled chicken salad with low-calorie dressing on the side and a Diet Coke.

"That's what I want, too," Kelly said, with a laugh.

Our similar tastes weren't limited to food.

While shopping in a large jewelry store in Jerusalem, I spotted a beautiful gold pendant with a smooth green stone in the center.

"It's a Jerusalem cross," the salesclerk explained. I fastened the necklace around my collar and admired it in the mirror. Just then, Kelly was by my side.

"That's the most beautiful one in the store," she remarked.

I turned to her and smiled. In her hands she held a box with the same necklace.

We laughed.

"Mind if I get one, too?" I asked.

"I think you should," she answered. "When we wear it, the necklace will not only remind us of our trip, but each other."

The necklaces became like sorority pins, signifying our connection to each other and our travel experience. Sharing the sights and sounds of the ancient land bonded us together. We rode camels in the desert, prayed at the Western Wall and floated in the salty water of the Dead Sea.

Halfway through the trip, our tour stopped at a kibbutz, a modest hostel just yards from the shores of the Sea of Galilee. That night when the room was dark, I confessed how disappointed I was that my marriage had failed.

"All my hopes and dreams were wrapped up in that relationship," I cried. "Now it's over."

Snuggled down in her twin bed, Kelly listened from the other side of the room.

"I see this not as an ending, but a beginning for you," she whispered.

Then I admitted my biggest fear.

"Even if I do meet someone, by the time we fall in love and get married, I'll be too old to have a baby."

Kelly was quiet a moment.

"You can't see it now, but I feel certain that you will remarry and have a child," she answered. "God has something wonderful in store for you—better than you can imagine."

"How can you say that? How do you know?" I wanted to believe her, but I felt so hopeless.

"I have faith," said Kelly.

Her words felt like a comforting blanket. Kelly held hope in her heart for me when I was too wounded to have it for myself.

The next morning on the bus, Kelly took my hand.

"I want to pray with you," she said.

I felt a bit uncomfortable, but I bowed my head and closed my eyes. Kelly discreetly asked God to give me faith to receive the life he had in store for me.

"Let's be prayer sisters," she suggested. "Each day we'll pray for each other and ask for God's blessings in life."

It sounded good to me. I needed all the prayers I could get. Kelly endeared herself as my prayer sister. By the time we left the Holy Land, we were as tight as biological sisters. Kelly's faith in my future gave me hope when I was too afraid to have it for myself.

That October, her beautiful son Chandler was born. Aunt Stephanie came to the hospital to take the first photos of the happy family. Even with the demands of motherhood, Kelly and I stayed close.

Throughout the years, I had dates, but never met anyone I was interested in. I gave up the hope of getting married, focused on work and felt content to live alone. Five years passed before I met and became friends with Michael. We fell deeply in love.

At forty years old, I married the man of my dreams on Valentine's Day. Kelly stood beside me that afternoon as Michael and I exchanged our vows.

The next morning, the doorbell rang incessantly. I opened the door to find on the porch a tray with a carafe of coffee, two personalized mugs, muffins, sausages, bacon, eggs, fresh fruit, snapshots from our wedding ceremony, two lit candles and a rose.

As I bent to bring in the feast, Kelly pulled out of the driveway, smiling and waving.

Later, I called to thank her.

"I've never stopped praying for this day," she said, softly. "I'm so happy for you."

Ten months afterward, I gave birth to my first child—a daughter, Micah Faith. She was named Micah for her father, Michael, and Faith for the unwavering belief in my future that Aunt Kelly had held for me so many years.

Yes, I believe God must have been in the kitchen that day in 1997. Only he could have served up a potluck roommate like Kelly, my best friend and the prayer sister who taught me to always have faith.

Stephanie Welcher Thompson

My Cup Runneth Over

I noticed a card on my coworker's desk. It was displayed for anyone to read. Still, not wanting to violate her privacy, I asked permission rather than just take the liberty. It was a birthday card from her sister—the kind that could only come from a sister.

The preprinted message was sweet, but the words written by her sister really struck me—like an arrow shot through the heart. The words moved me deeply, both because of their beautiful sentiment and the fact that I had lost my one and only sister—not to death, but to the ravages of mental illness, and with it, the insidious annihilation of her mind.

My sister, eighteen months older than I, became ill at the age of nineteen. It was just about the time that sisters really start to connect and discard the childish "That's my shirt; you can't wear it!" and "Don't touch my stuff, you little brat." I watched other sisters grow into friends and confidantes. I watched my sister digress as our relationship disintegrated into caregiver/patient. It has torn me apart a little piece at a time over the last three decades. She's been gone longer than I had her. I'm amazed to find that there are still sharp, little shards of broken heart left to scratch at my insides.

Any nostalgia we could've shared from our childhood is lost and forever locked up in her mind along with her soul. Often I mourn the loss of that one relationship and what could've been. How I long to have my sister back. I miss her and feel cheated by her condemnation.

I coveted the words in my coworker's card. Her sister wrote, "Our parents did a lot, if not most things, wrong. But the one thing they did right was give me sisters. I am eternally grateful for you." I held back the tears. I told her how lucky she was to have a sister, one like that anyway. I was jealous.

Her eyes grew wide incredulously, as if to ask how I could be jealous. She motioned toward my proudly displayed collection of keepsake cards and pictures. You know the kind—the ones you read over and over again for sustenance and comfort when everything that can go wrong does. The ones that assuage and soothe the psyche like a tight, lingering hug or the warm cup of milk my grandma gave me whenever anything ailed me.

She was perplexed at my jealousy since she'd already read every card on my desk. All dozen or so came from my two best friends, Imelda and Gopali. Each and every one had been signed "with love, from your sister." She presumed they were my sisters. She went on to say that she finally displayed a card of her own because, at long last, she got one from her own sister that was as poignant as those on my desk—the ones she had secretly envied.

We burst into spontaneous laughter, and then we talked and connected in a way we hadn't before. I explained about my sister and the sadness and loss I suffered. How I ached for that special connection that was ripped from me some thirty years before. That I felt cheated by the world and by my sister's life sentence. How my big sister, and therefore parts of me, were locked away forever in the recesses of her imprisoned mind. How guilty I felt for feeling sorry for myself when my sister's loss far outweighed my own. It wasn't fair.

She looked at me most solemnly and said, "If those two women are not your sisters, then I don't know who is." And sad as it is to have lost a sister, I was more than fortunate to have gained two. Just because we were not biologically connected, they are no less my sisters than a mother is to her adopted child. She called them soul sisters. And while blood is thicker than water, souls are like glue, thicker still and the stuff of which unbreakable bonds are made. These women are indeed my sisters.

This woman helped me realize that I'd been seeing this half-empty glass when the reality was that my cup runneth over. I don't feel cheated anymore. In fact, I've made a new friend. Actually, I've found another sister.

Kim McClean Sullivan

6

SPECIAL MEMORIES

The best thing about having a sister is that I always had a friend.

Cali Rae Turner

Lessons from the Past

Let us not love with words or tongue but with actions and in truth.

I John 3:18

As a young married woman, my husband's grandmother, Aetna, endured part of the Great Depression in the desolate area of northern Alberta, Canada. Fortunately, two of her sisters, Julie and Nora, also lived nearby.

One year, as Christmas approached, Aetna managed to save one dollar to spend on presents for her three daughters. Julie had scrimped enough to provide gifts for her four children, as well. Both women looked forward to Christmas morning when their little ones would open their presents from Santa Claus. They were just small items, like a harmonica, a hair ribbon or a set of ball-and-jacks, but during those bleak times these seemed like treasures.

Christmas in Nora's house, however, was going to be different. She had nine children. No matter how much Nora and her husband, Alf, worked and saved, when

Christmas came, they could not afford presents for the children. They didn't even have food for Christmas dinner.

On Christmas Eve, Nora and Alf gathered their children around them.

"I'm sorry," Alf said, "but Santa Claus isn't coming this year."

The children were crestfallen. "Why not?" asked Lorne, one of the boys.

Alf stared at the floor. "He's just not. He can't."

Later, as Nora tucked the disappointed children into bed, Alf sat at the kitchen table, buried his head in his hands and sobbed. That was where Aetna and Julie found him when they walked through the door. In their arms they carried a box of small presents, several dishes of food, one butterscotch pie and exactly one-half of a turkey.

Earlier that evening, Julie had hurried to Aetna's house with the news of Nora and Alf's situation. The women immediately set to work. Aetna and Julie took one present from each of their children to give to Nora's children, plus a couple more to equal nine. They divided the contents of their Christmas dinners to share with Nora. Aetna had baked two butterscotch pies, so Nora got one. But since there was only one turkey, Aetna sawed it down the middle and wrapped up half for her sister's family.

Aetna and Julie packed up everything and walked together through the wintry Alberta night to their sister's house. There they, Alf and Nora set up a small tree, decorated it with foil and hung the children's presents from the boughs.

The next morning, Nora and Alf's children stumbled out of bed. When they saw the Christmas tree laden with presents for them, Lorne exclaimed, "He did come!"

That was surely the best gift Aetna and Julie gave to their sister—the preservation of her child's belief in miracles.

Even during such meager times as the Great Depression, the sisters never hesitated to show generosity to each other. Whatever they had, they shared. No sister expected thanks; she knew that next time it might be she who was in need.

But she also knew she would never be alone in it.

Kristin Walker

The Blue Tree

It had been about a year since my sister died. We had been about as close as sisters could be—always sharing, talking and even arguing as sisters do. As young women we had shared our dreams and fears with each other. We were both believers in God, but we had an equal fear of death and the afterlife . . . never completely trusting in our faith, but searching for some sort of proof and reassurance.

When my sister fell ill at the age of nineteen, we never dreamed that her illness would be terminal. She was so young and full of life, excelling in college with a bright future ahead of her. Years later, we were to discover that the illness she had been fighting was AIDS, and that it was certain that her life would be cut short. Throughout her illness, her fear of the afterlife began to diminish.

I was at her side when she died at the age of twenty-nine, and although she did not want to leave her family, she expressed no doubts about her place in heaven and the beauty that awaited her. I, however, still wanted some reassurance . . . I wanted proof. For a year, I looked for signs daily from my sister. I looked at the world through different eyes. Every bird . . . every butterfly . . . I would wait for them to land on my windowsill with some message, some recognition and proof of the afterlife.

It was then that I dreamed of my sister. She was alive and healthy, and we shared and talked as though she were right beside me. We talked of my need for proof of heaven and eternal life, and she smiled and said, "Sweetie, just look for the blue tree. . . . It will help show you what life is all about . . . and reassure you of God and heaven. Just look for the blue tree." I woke up that morning and told my family about my dream. My mother, having been devastated by the loss of a child, also clung to any signs of my sister's afterlife in heaven. We discussed the improbability of ever seeing a blue tree. . . . Was there such a thing? And if there were a blue tree, how would it all make sense?

Days later after a long week at work, I was home with my family. My children were settling down for the night, and we had all gathered in the living room to read a bedtime story. My three-year-old daughter, Madison, had always had a very special bond with her Aunt Laura before her death. That night Madison said that she wanted to "read" to everyone, and she crawled up into my lap and began her story. I remember feeling the love in the room. It wasn't very often that we could stop our hectic lives just to sit together and share. My daughter began to fumble through a Dr. Seuss book, reciting the words she had memorized, when she looked up at me with her hands around my neck and said, "Mommy, look . . . a blue tree. A red dog in a blue tree." And right then I knew . . . my sister had sent me a sign. My proof had been right in front of me all along.

It was all about family and love and children. That was my proof of God's existence . . . the blue tree.

Meredith Robnett

The Day My Sister Mailed Herself Away

Mom intended to savor the box of chocolates Dad bought her for Valentine's Day clear into March! She kept her giant two-pound box under her bed. "I'm just eating one a day. I want them to last. You kids stay out of them! I may let you have one every so often, but that's all. I'd better not catch anyone in them! Did you kids hear me?"

"Yes, Mom," we promised, as convincingly as we could. A few days later, the promise was broken.

"Glenda and LaVelle, get in here!" she called from her bedroom. "There should have only been three or four chocolates gone, and the entire top layer is gone! That comes to one pound! Which one of you little whelps did this?" I knew I didn't, so I told Mom that LaVelle did.

"No, I didn't eat them. A little mouse must have ate the whole bunch, Mama," LaVelle declared, hoping she could blame the mouse Mom was always setting a trap for.

I could see the twinkle of laughter in Mom's eyes, but LaVelle didn't. LaVelle didn't see one iota of hilarity in the whole situation because she thought she would be spanked or made to go to bed without dinner. She was too young to be grounded or have to do the dishes for a month.

"I'm going to think until this afternoon about how I will discipline you. Now, you think about what you did."

There was no escape. LaVelle decided in her five-year-old mind to mail herself to Grandma. She knew when the hands of the clock were on a one and a zero that it was time for the mailman to pick up the mail.

It was 9:30 A.M. and a cold, snowy March morning. LaVelle put on her snowsuit and walked out the door. It was a long road to the main highway. Little did she know she was about to become a family legend.

Close to 10:00 A.M., Mom began to have a worry-wonder sound in her voice. "Do you know where LaVelle is?"

"No, Mom," I said, sensing this was not a time to make up a story.

"She must be hiding because she knows I'm going to give her a punishment."

I ran to all the places I thought she would hide in. I peeked in the laundry chute and looked under all the beds, in the lower kitchen cabinets, behind the clothes in Mom and Dad's closet, and even behind the big pile in the laundry room. I ran outside to Dad's shop without even putting on a coat. She wasn't there. I ran back in the house screaming at the top of my lungs, "Mom, LaVelle's gone! She's really gone!"

Mom became frantic. I looked out the window and saw her running toward Dad's shop screaming, "Lloyd! Lloyd!"

A few seconds later, Mom and Dad were both back in the house. "I'm calling the police," Dad said.

"Oh, dear God! What if she's lost in the woods? She will freeze to death!" Mom cried.

I started to sob. Just then the phone rang.

Dad answered it and listened with a shocked look. We all expected the worst until Dad said, "Thank you, Maudie. We'll be right there." Then he burst out laughing.

"That was the post office in Rhododendron. They have

a package for us. It's LaVelle! The mailman found her sitting by the mailbox in the snowbank as he stopped to get our mail. He asked her what she was doing so far from home, and she told him she was 'mailing myself away.' When he asked her why, she said, 'Because I ate almost all of Mama's chocolates, and I may get a spanking.'"

"What! She mailed herself away!" Mom screamed in disbelief. I sat frozen in shock.

"I'll warm up the car. Let's both go, Margorie." Dad chuckled again.

I watched them from the front window as they drove out to the road. I pictured my sister getting spanked amongst all the packages at the post office.

Soon they were back. The first thing I noticed was the postage stamp stuck to the center of my sister's forehead. I couldn't take my eyes off it because it was so different from a gold star.

"They gave me hot cocoa," she stated proudly.

"I should give you a spanking," Mama answered, "but I'm not going to because I'm so glad to see you. For some reason, your daddy thinks this whole thing is soooo funny. I don't see anything funny about you worrying Mama so much that her stomach hurts!"

Later, at dinner, my sister told her version of the story.

"The nice mailman said he would take me to the post office to see how many stamps it would take to mail me to Grandma's. When we got to the post office, the nice mailman asked Maudie how many stamps it would take. Maudie said, 'We don't have enough stamps. She has to be stamped for bringing her here.' Then she put this stamp on my forehead."

Daddy started laughing again. "Daddy wants to take your picture by the mailbox tomorrow so we can put it in the album. We don't want to forget this, do we, Margorie?" he said, and he laughed again. Mom even kind of smiled.

That night, as Mom tucked her in, I saw her kiss my little sister—right on top of the postage stamp, still stuck to her forehead.

Glenda Barbre

The Night the Attic Floor Creaked

"All right, children," Mother said, tucking my big sister, Betty, and me in under a pile of homemade quilts. "Get to sleep. If Santa Claus finds you awake, he just might not leave you anything."

I shivered at the dreadful thought. "Nothing at all?"

Mother smiled. "Well, he likes the house to be perfectly still. And all the boys and girls sound asleep. Remember when you told Santa what you wanted? Okay, lights out."

She kissed us and picked up the old kerosene lamp. In a moment, our little bedroom was pitch black.

Oh, I did believe in Santa. I believed in him with my whole heart! The thought of displeasing him by letting him find me awake was terrifying. *What if he did decide not to leave my doll, after all?* I shut my eyes as tightly as possible and pulled the covers over my head.

"Psst, Bonnie!" My sister Betty moved over from her side of the big bed and nudged me.

I kicked her under the covers. "Shh! Santa might hear you!"

She giggled. "What?" she whispered back in her already-eight-practically-grown-up voice. "You don't really believe all that stuff, do you?"

"Of course, I do! Now, shh! He'll hear you."

"Bonnie! There's not room up on our roof for a sleigh, much less Santa and all those reindeer. Besides, they'd be so heavy they'd crash right through. And besides"—not even hiding her scorn—"Daddy locks the front and back doors every night. How do you think Santa would get in?"

Now it was my turn for scorn. "The chimney, stupid. Don't you remember?"

"Maybe for houses that have fireplaces. But if he came down *our* chimney, he'd land smack in the middle of our potbellied stove!"

"He came last year, smarty, didn't he? And the year before? So he got in here somehow!"

My sister stifled a horsy laugh. "*Someone* got here. But not necessarily Santa!"

"What do you mean?"

"Wait a few minutes, keep your ears open, and you'll find out for yourself."

By now our farmhouse was still. My three-year-old brother, Bobby, was curled up on his little cot. Paula, the baby, snuggled in her crib. The fire in the woodstove had turned to embers. The animals out in the barn had settled down for the night.

Suddenly, I heard exactly what I was waiting for—creaks and footsteps—right over my head!

"Betty!" I whispered, nudging her. "Hear that? That's Santa's sleigh!"

"What makes you think so?" she sneered.

"Don't you hear that noise on the roof? And those feet? You can hear his voice, too. Oh, boy, I hope he didn't forget my doll!" In horror, "Betty, don't you dare start giggling! He'll hear you!"

But she was laughing so hard that she had to stuff the pillow in her mouth. "Shh, yourself," she hiccupped. "So what's he saying?"

I stood up on our bed and stretched up as high as I could to catch the sounds of this magical moment. And what I heard was—*my own father's voice.*

Still, I resisted. "That means he's helping Santa."

Betty yawned. "Oh, pshaw! That means he and Mother *are* Santa. Now grow up and accept it."

I thought I would never get to sleep after that, especially a little later as I listened to Daddy hammer and screw something in the living room.

But I guess I did sleep after all, for next thing I knew Betty was shaking me. "Come on, sleepyhead! It's Christmas morning!"

We raced into the freezing living room. The candles and kerosene lamp were out, and the fire not started, but we could see glorious boxes and bags all over. Even lumpy stockings stuffed to the top!

"Let's wake up Mother and Daddy!" I urged. "Wait till they see what Santa brought."

"I think they've already seen it," she replied dryly. But in a minute, we were all on our parents' bed. "It's Christmas!" Betty shouted, as Mother and Daddy rubbed their weary eyes. "Come see what Santa brought!"

I stared at her. "*Santa?* But last night you said—"

"Oh, hush!" she said. "Forget what I said. It's Christmas!"

And so it was. A glorious Christmas. Our stockings were crammed with nuts and apples we'd picked ourselves in the fall, plus the most beautiful pieces of hard candy I'd ever seen. Their colors glistened like jewels! They had centers like Christmas trees and Santas and stars. And, yes! I even got five Hershey's Kisses. *Five!*

And I got a pencil and a big yellow tablet. And a doll. A real baby doll, with eyes that opened and shut, all wrapped up cozy in a little blanket Mother had sewn just for her, edged in blue ribbon—my favorite color. I named her Princess Patty. Betty's doll had a blanket, too—with red ribbons—her favorite color. We put our dolls in Bobby's new red wagon along with our baby sister Paula, and we all took turns pulling the wagon around the house and generally making a joyful racket.

"You were right about last night," I told Betty later. "Mother and Daddy did give us our dolls, not Santa Claus. Santa could never have sewn a blanket for my doll half as good as Mother."

She grinned and held out her half-empty stocking. "Want to trade three Santa Claus faces for a Kiss?"

Suddenly businesslike, I looked in my own bag. "Maybe. Throw in three nuts, and it's a deal."

Just then Daddy came in. "I like Kisses, too," he teased, holding out his hand.

So he got kisses—a lot of them. The mushy, hug-and-hold kind.

But not the Hershey ones. If he wanted some of those, he should have asked Santa himself!

Bonnie Compton Hanson

Road Trip Down Memory Lane

How good it is to have a sister whose heart is as young as your own.

Pam Brown

There's a wonderful nightclub scene in the movie *White Christmas* when Rosemary Clooney sings about her especially close relationship with her sister. Like many close-knit families, my sisters and I believe that those famous Irving Berlin lyrics could have been written about us.

Among the three of us, we account for eighty-five years of marriage, eight children, four pets, four mortgages and three full-time jobs. (The total number of pounds we weigh will remain our little secret.) Given our hectic lives, when my oldest sister suggested a "sisters-only" visit to our father in Florida, coming up with a mutually convenient time for our road trip was no easy task. Although planning the trip was the hard part, the easy part was what we discovered, and rediscovered, along the way.

While preparing for our visit, we pulled out a favorite black-and-white photo of the three of us in matching swimsuits, blissfully eating vanilla ice-cream pops with our dad at Orchard Beach in the Bronx. Although we no longer had matching bathing suits for the sisters' outing to Florida, we did still share an immense sense of joy in life's simple pleasures—a clear blue sky, amazing seashells, and the wonderful smell of the fresh, salty air. As we waded together into the water on Nakomis Beach, the years rolled out with the tide.

Throughout the trip, family memories arose in unexpected places. One Sunday morning, we all piled into my father's red sedan to take a ride. We dutifully fastened our seat belts before taking off, but when we approached a stop sign and the car stopped abruptly, my sister in the front seat flung her arm out and yelled "hang on"—a reminder of what had passed for "seat belts" when we were children! Moving out onto the open road, safely secured in our seats, we belted out the oldies as the highway signs—and time—flew by.

That same afternoon we had an opportunity to tour a new home development and fantasize about the million-dollar palaces our wealthy "next" husbands would buy us. As we exited one resort, a tall, handsome man was just returning to his home on the premises. As he passed out of earshot, I heard a familiar refrain often whispered during our teenaged years . . . "I saw him first!"

Later that night, huddled in one of the spare bedrooms, we called up one of our "real" husbands and pretended to be interested in an item he was selling on eBay. We thought we sounded completely believable—but the giggling in the background must have given us away.

As we prepared for our farewell pajama party, congratulating ourselves on what perfect guests we were, our words were punctuated by a loud crash. In horror we realized that the noise was the Murphy bed announcing its intention to retire from further service. (Honestly, we were not singing *three little monkeys jumping on the bed* at the time of its demise.) After a stunned silence, we leaped into action. In what could have passed for an early episode of *I Love Lucy*, we struggled to push the Murphy bed back into the wall. No luck. We then lugged the mattress off the iron frame and propped it up against the sliding door—all the while hoping it wouldn't crash through the door and wake our father! With the mattress precariously balanced against the door, we fussed and fiddled with the Murphy bed frame, but still no luck. As a last resort, I volunteered to climb into the Murphy bed closet while my two sisters tried to raise the bed. (Who says the youngest child is spoiled?) Despite our best efforts—we really could have used the muscle of the husbands and sons we left behind—we had to concede that we were no match for the stubborn Mr. Murphy.

Although we have 158 years of age among us, we spent the rest of the night worrying that *"Ohmygod, Dad is going to kill us!"* Morning dawned, and, of course, no one was murdered. Even Murphy couldn't dampen our father's joy at having his daughters together.

Our short-term memories aren't what they once were—throughout the visit we misplaced reading glasses and cell phones with regularity—but thankfully our long-term sister memories are still very much alive.

Pamela Hackett Hobson

Half Notes: Memories of a Fifty-Percent Sister

If love could be measured, it would be measured by how much it gives.

Joni Eareckson Tada

I am a sister. And I'm an only child. Confused? Actually, to understand my family and my place in it, you need to see the movie, *Yours, Mine and Ours*. When I was a child in the sixties, I saw the first version of this movie with Lucille Ball and Henry Fonda, and it gave me a glimmer of hope. After seeing the film, I realized that I wasn't alone in my family mishmash. There could be other family trees out there in the world as pruned and propagated as mine.

In the movie, Lucy and Henry are a lonely widow and widower, each with a bunch of kids—that's where the *yours* and *mine* come in. The two marry and have a child who is the *ours* in the story. I am an *ours*. And I'm the half-sister to five siblings.

My family's version of the flick goes like this: Dad's first wife died of cancer, leaving behind two grieving sons and a daughter. Mother's first husband took his own life, not thinking of the painful legacy he was leaving for two dark-haired daughters. The widower and widow met at the Tabernacle Methodist Church carry-in dinner. They married and combined their families—which, in 1957, was very un-*Leave-It-to-Beaver*. Ward would have swallowed his pipe.

I discovered I was a half-sister when I was five years old, and a friend asked me how many sisters and brothers I had. I hesitated because by then all of my siblings were out of the house, married or in college. So I asked my mother how many siblings I had. "You have five *half*-brothers and -sisters," Mother said.

"Half?" I muttered. The last time I saw them, they looked to be in one piece.

"That means they are half-related to you," Mother explained.

"Denny, Becky, Joann, Kathy and Jackie aren't whole brothers and sisters?" I asked, stunned.

"No, they're just half," Mother said.

That couldn't be true, I thought. My brothers and sisters felt like complete relatives to me, no matter what Mother said.

I thought back to the day before my mother dropped the half-sister bomb on my kindergarten world. Twenty-year-old Denny and I had played Old Maid on the living-room floor. Later, he tickled me until I rolled off the couch laughing. *If that wasn't a full brother*, I thought, *I would like to know what is.*

Growing up, I had repeatedly heard the story that my youngest sister, Becky, who was fourteen when I was born, was so excited to hear our mother was pregnant with me that on her way home from school, she bought Mother a pickle at S. S. Kresgee. At Christmas, Jackie drove me around town to look at holiday lights. In the spring,

Kathy helped me plant flower seeds in tin cans. Joann taught me how to sing, "Won't You Come Home, Bill Bailey?" All of that was *half*?

Soon after I learned I was a half-sister, my playmate, blonde Sherry Jackson, asked me if I was the oldest or the youngest kid in my family. All of my newly learned half-sibling information swirled in my head. How should I answer? I'm the youngest, but in a way I'm the only. How could I tell her I was fifty percent of a sister? Blonde Sherry Jackson had it all—an older, 100-percent-related, blonde sister and a younger, entirely related equally-as-blonde sister. Blonde Sherry Jackson probably never even heard of a half-sister. I'd be speaking some foreign, half-sister tongue if I attempted to explain my family to her.

I have wrestled with how to explain my family my entire life. Today, people would say that I'm part of a "blended" family—a term not yet coined when my parents threw their children into the Mixmaster formed by their union and poured out a new household of kin.

I was the addition each person in my family could claim as theirs, and that was always a good feeling for me. I am the only family member who is a blood relative of the other seven. Yet, it can seem like a burdensome responsibility. Being an *ours* can be a lonely experience, perhaps lonelier than being an only. With an only child there's no family dynamics of half-siblings, stepchildren, step-parents, stepdogs.

I accepted all of my family, the halves and the half-nots, the steps and the stepped on. For me, there was never a before and after. My half-siblings knew a time before their parents died, the misery of the days after their parents passed on, then the adjustment when their surviving parent remarried. They watched me come into this world, brandishing two complete parents and a roster of half-siblings.

I heard stories of the deceased parents—the mystery

dad and the "ghost" mother, loved before my time by my parents and my siblings. My "halves" had uncles, aunts and cousins who were theirs alone. I'd ask my mother, "Is Lois related to me?"

"Not really," Mother would explain. "She's Denny, Kathy and Jackie's cousin."

At times, I felt some jealousy from some of my siblings because I had both of my parents and, in my siblings' eyes, I had an easier childhood. (But often the baby in the family has an easier upbringing, regardless of her bloodline.)

Sometimes it's difficult for people with "traditional" families to understand my sibling soup. They want to differentiate my brothers and sisters from the full-blooded variety. They say, "She's your *half*-sister, right?" Even with our dysfunction and divisions (the ugly stuff that's part of all families), I rarely label my brothers and sisters "half-brother" or "half-sister" because, in my heart, if I did, I'd be downgrading all that they mean to me. And I'd be left fifty-percent of a sister.

All of my life, half has been as whole as I could hope for.

Angie Klink

Turn Off the Light

I tell you there is one thing that draws above everything else in the world and that is love.

D. L. Moody

Imagine a family of eight residing in a dreary, little two-bedroom house with a condemnation notice. That was our temporary living arrangement while Dad completed a transfer with his railroad job, moving his family closer to the city they knew and loved. We were the last renters at the house before it met its demise, and we made liberal use of that opportunity. We literally wrote on the walls, covering the drab gray wallpaper with colorful drawings and thoughts about the old house. ("This wallpaper stinks!")

It was an odd little house, with a bathroom right off the kitchen. Space was limited, and the bathroom doubled as a pantry for canned goods. There was another bathroom upstairs, but with eight people, sometimes you had to wait for your soup. The stairway to the upper floor had a banister railing. We kids never did descend the stairs; we rode the banister. We slid down with glee, even though it would occasionally leave small black streaks on our shirts. We'd wear them with pride.

My two brothers shared a bedroom, and we four sisters shared the other, with Mom and Dad relegated to the hide-a-bed sofa in the living room. We managed to fit two bunk beds in our small bedroom, leaving enough walking space between them and not much else. We taped pictures of Scott Baio and Willie Aames to our walls, and any other cuties from the latest teen magazine. You had to be careful what you wrote on the walls, though, especially after a fight with a sibling—there was no hiding the evidence (unless you got another teen magazine).

Sharing a room with three sisters, there may have been an argument or two. Mostly it was about who would turn off the light at bedtime after we were all tucked in. There was no light fixture, just a bulb dangling from the middle of the ceiling with one of those metal ball strings attached. Simple enough, yet no one wanted to get out of bed to turn it off. We would lay there in the glare of the room and chant, "Turn off the light! Turn off the light!" All of us would join in, laughing, until we'd hear our brothers or parents yell at us to turn off the darn light and go to bed. My younger sister, Jen, and I had the bottom bunks, and we usually had to do the turning off just by default of our youth. Our older sisters, Mary and Annie, had top bunks, thereby securing some lofty position of authority in the room.

When Jen and I whined loudly enough about always having to turn off the light, we changed the rule to last one in bed had to turn off the light. Four of us at once jostled up the stairs, vying for best spot at the bathroom sink to brush our teeth (for all of five seconds), and then scrambled into bed. Inevitably, Jen and I still ended up being the last ones in bed. We whined about this, too. When our bellyaching reached fever pitch, it prompted action.

Mary and Annie devised a simple solution—a piece of string tied from the light bulb's metal-ball string to the bedpost that with one quick tug turned off the darn light. We were proud of our rudimentary physics. It saved endless fights about who had turned out the light the most times, and it was someone else's turn because eighty-seven times was the limit for one person. Of course, the string system did not end our ritual of chanting, "Turn off the light! Turn off the light!" It just made it more fun with our homemade remote.

The old house is since gone, and a few more rooms have been shared with my younger sister, Jen. Modern light fixtures forbade use of our string technique, and I usually pulled rank and made Jen turn off the light. We'd lay in our bunks in the darkness, neither wanting to be the first to drift off, when one of us would whisper, "Turn off the light! Turn off the light!" The other would join in, and giggles would follow.

All four of us sisters are married now, graduating from bunk beds to queens and kings to be shared with husbands. The light issue is resolved at my house by a remote control. But I'm wondering about my sisters' houses and imagining them chanting to their husbands, "Turn off the light! Turn off the light!" And laughing.

Becky Alban

Every Rose Has Its Thorns

Siblings are the people who teach us about fairness and cooperation and kindness and caring—quite often the hard way.

Pamela Dugdale

She was the light of my life, my baby sister, Kathy. She was the last of my mother's six children. Maybe that's why Mom didn't protest too much when, at age thirteen, I took over much of her care as an infant. I fed her, diapered her, played with her and sang to her. I carried her around the circle in our house, through the living room, dining room and hallway, to put her to sleep every night.

At around the age of three or four, Kathy developed a sinister streak . . . an obsession with tormenting our animals, especially the cats. One day my brother went out to feed his rabbits and found Sonny, our male cat, locked up in one of the rabbit cages. On another occasion, we heard a faint meowing and followed the sound to the potbellied stove my mom used as a planter on the front porch. There, shut inside the stove, was Cher, Sonny's counterpart. Kathy confessed to the crimes. I lectured her about the importance of being kind to the animals, and all was forgiven.

Now when I saw Kathy looking over the edge of the large concrete watering trough in the barnyard, I had to be a bit suspicious. I walked over to find three baby chicks flailing in the water, fighting for all they were worth to stay afloat. As I fished them out, I asked Kathy why she had done that. Her simple reply was, "I wanted to see if they could swim."

Needless to say, my frustrations with her antics were mounting. I had to find a way to impart my love of animals to her, to make her understand that animals are living things that hurt just like we do.

God . . . and sisters . . . truly do work in mysterious ways.

A short time after the incident with the swimming chicks, I walked out the back door just in time to see Kathy throw one of the cats into the rosebushes at the edge of the porch. Without a hesitant thought, I picked her up and threw her in right after it, then profoundly stated, "Don't you ever do to an animal what you wouldn't want done to you!"

Of course, after I realized what I had just done and seen the look of surprise and then hurt on her face, I quickly scooped her up, told her I was sorry and pulled the thorns out of her arms, legs and rear.

For many years, I felt guilty about having done such a dreadful thing to my baby sister until one day when we were both all grown up, sitting on the steps at her house and petting her dog. With a half-wink, an impish smile and a mocking rub of her behind, Kathy said to me, "I have you to thank for my love of animals, you know."

Luanna K. Warner

"She's cute. We'll be able to find her a good home."

The Green Colander

Happiness is not a station you arrive at, but a manner of traveling.

Cecil Murphey

Every day after school in May, my sister and I would get off the school bus and trudge down the long gravel driveway. Neither one of us would be in a hurry because we knew what usually awaited: the green colander. Mom would take our school bags and, in exchange, hand us a lime-green plastic colander. That meant we had to go fill it with asparagus for dinner.

I was usually tired and grumpy after school, and all I wanted was to be left alone. Somehow having to do this chore was all my sister's fault. Why couldn't she go pick the stuff by herself? I kind of liked eating the asparagus, especially with cheese sauce, but raw asparagus is filled with disgustingly stinky juice. When you put fresh asparagus in that colander, eventually the smelly stuff would drip out through the holes. It took a lot of scrubbing to get that smell off your hands.

My sister and I would fight over who had to carry the

colander. Somehow it usually ended up being me, maybe because I was oldest. After that issue was decided, we'd march off through the backyard and out into the field behind the house. Our house was built on a piece of old farmland, and the back field was full of about an acre of asparagus some farmer had planted that still came up year after year. I'd take one side of the field, and my sister would take the other.

Through that field I'd stomp, eyes searching the tall grasses for the asparagus sprouts hiding beneath. When I found one, I'd snap it off with my hand, and into the colander it would go. Besides keeping an eye out for potential pickings, I'd keep an eye on my sister to be sure she wasn't slacking off. If we didn't come back with enough asparagus, Mom would send us out again, and I wasn't about to do all the work. Sometimes I'd cheat and pick even the stalks that had started to go a little wild, breaking off the tiny, sprouting branches so the stalk looked more like a smooth new shoot. Some stalks were so fat and old they were as thick as my wrist. Those needed two hands to snap off, and I'd tackle them angrily just to show them who was boss, even though they didn't count for dinner. Every so often I'd meet my sister in the middle of the field, and into the colander she'd dump her haul.

One day I angrily snapped off one of those big, old shoots that had started to go to seed. It had grown about a foot long or more and was too far gone to be added to the colander as a cheater stalk. I glanced over at my sister, and she had her back to me as she was searching for shoots in the grass. I held that thick, old stalk and whacked some of the tall grasses with it. That old asparagus felt like a wiggly, old stick. Suddenly, a wicked idea grew. Before I could think about it, I threw that old stalk as far across the field as I could. It went careening through the air, spinning and spinning like a wobbly green baton. It missed my sister, but hit the grass beside her with a swish. She froze in alarm, staring at the spot where she heard the noise. I quickly bent down and pretended to be doing my job. My sides shook with laughter.

That was such a good trick to play on her that I did it again. I missed once more, but my aim was getting better. Again I faked my search for more spears while waiting for another chance to try my aim. Suddenly, a big, old stalk came whizzing through the air. It narrowly missed my head! That did it. I burst out laughing and could hear my sister doing the same. For the next few minutes it was every sister for herself. We raced from tall, old stalk to tall, old stalk, quickly snapping them off and launching them across the field at each other, the colander all but forgotten. Finally, we were panting with exhaustion and had used up all the old asparagus close at hand. Quickly and quietly, we resumed our colander-filling quest.

From then on, it became a game to surprise the other with an airborne asparagus when her back was turned. Sometimes we'd actually make contact, but even if I missed, it was still funny to see her freeze for a moment, trying to decide whether the swish in the grass was an asparagus or a startled snake or mouse running for cover. For many years to follow, even as our youngest sister became old enough to join in the picking, the sight of that after-school green colander was still cause for grumbling, but at least it had also become the chance for a rematch.

Lizann Flatt

Five Miles of Paper for Ten Dollars

A family is a unit composed not only of children, but of men, women, an occasional animal and the common cold.

Ogden Nash

Picture in your head a Christmas morning. Four little towheaded boys are sneaking down the stairs to see what Santa has brought for them. And what to their wondering eyes should appear? Bright, fluorescent orange. There are piles of shiny orange packages everywhere. There are no pretty boxes wrapped with chubby snowmen or gaily painted reindeer—just glossy orange. "Santa must like the color orange," the smallest child remarks. No cute angels, toy soldiers or candy canes patterned with stripes adorn the wrapping—just plain orange. Yes, this is a house in America, and this isn't a weird ritual or unusual ethnic custom. Welcome to Susie's house in New Jersey.

My dear sister-in-law, Susie, is the type of person who livens up any room she enters. When she married my brother, Howard, thirty years ago, I acquired another sister. As we raised our families together, she enriched my life in many ways with her vibrant personality.

Susie always had an eye for a bargain, and she hit the jackpot the day she stopped at a small roadside flea market. A vendor was selling large rolls of bright orange Mylar paper for only ten dollars. When she asked the vendor the length of the paper, he responded, "Lady, there must be five miles of this stuff on these rolls."

"Wow, this will make great wrapping paper," Susie whispered to herself. With four sons of her own and many nieces and nephews, she saw this purchase as a way to cut costs.

For years, birthday and anniversary presents arrived wrapped in the familiar carrot-tinted paper. When our families assembled to exchange Christmas presents, there was no need for Susie to attach labels to her presents. "I know who gave me this one," someone would invariably say as they opened their fluorescent package. For years and years, those vividly colored presents brightened our holidays. We all wondered when Susie's kids made the connection that Santa used the same paper to wrap presents that their mom did.

The famous expression, "Sometimes you don't really appreciate things till you don't have them anymore" rang true for our family a few years ago. After years of chiding Susie with the perennial joking question, "How much of that paper do you have left anyway?" the bright orange presents stopped. Susie and her family had moved to a larger house to accommodate the growing boys. Somehow between the cleaning, packing and moving, the paper disappeared. We wondered if some lucky soul had the good fortune to find the paper, maybe in a trash can somewhere, and retrieve it for her family. Life moved on, the kids grew up, and holidays came and went. Whether caused by the newfound interests of the children or the lack of that brilliant paper, our family gatherings were becoming duller; something was missing.

This past Christmas, Susie and her family arrived at our home, laden with presents as usual. When they opened the bags carrying the gifts, we were treated to a great surprise—bright orange everywhere! Orange boxes of assorted shapes and sizes tumbled out. "Where did you find the paper?" I squealed with delight.

"Believe it or not," Susie said, "I found it under Steven's bed." Steven is her eldest son and, simply stated, he was never known for his housekeeping abilities. Steven had sworn to his mother, "I had no idea it was under my bed, Mom, honest."

That crazy fluorescent paper was a gift itself. It served as a wonderful memory of past good times shared with family, some who were no longer with us. Excitedly, I asked Susie how much paper she had left and, happily, for our whole family, she replied, "Don't worry, there are at least two miles left!"

Susan Siersma

The Longest Night

There is no substitute for the comfort supplied by the utterly taken-for-granted relationship.

Iris Murdoch

Science may say that the summer solstice is the longest day of the year, but any child knows that the longest day of the year falls on Christmas Eve. For my brother, sister and me, the hours on this day crawled by at a snail's pace. While Mama bustled about the house, cleaning and preparing a veritable feast for the next day's gathering, we whiled away the hours pestering her relentlessly.

"Mama, what time is it?"

"Mama, how much longer until nighttime?"

"Mama, when will Santa get here?"

All day long, we waited, trying desperately to be kind and patient, for we knew that Santa was watching more closely than ever. Though we attempted to busy ourselves with games and activities, the day passed much too slowly.

One year, however, Christmas Eve passed more quickly than usual, for the three of us were reaching the age when our curiosity about jolly Saint Nicholas was irrepressible. Was the man in the red-velvet suit real or merely a figment of our imaginations? We determined that the time had come for us to prove or disprove his existence. For once, Mama was able to dust, vacuum, chop and simmer without interruption because her three children were hidden away upstairs plotting and planning. We were going to trap Santa!

All that long day, we prepared for our midnight attack. Every detail and each strategy was discussed, written down on a tattered piece of lined notebook paper, erased and then rewritten. We stashed rope and flashlights and devised the story that we would tell Mama and Daddy so that we could all sleep in the same room, the room nearest the stairs. We planned our reconnaissance missions and tried in vain to tie lassos and slipknots, for our intention was to capture Santa and, with any luck at all, a reindeer or two!

By the time that evening arrived, we were itching with anticipation. Never before have three youngsters wanted to go to bed so early. It was time for Phase One of our plan to be put into action—sleeping arrangements. We painted on our sweetest and most innocent smiles and approached Mama and Daddy.

"Mama," asked my older sister, "may we all sleep in Skipper's room tonight?"

"Yeah," said my brother. "That way you won't have to make up so many beds in the morning." His smile broadened.

"And we promise to go right to sleep," I proclaimed. The invisible halo perched atop my golden tresses barely wobbled.

Mama and Daddy glanced at each other. "I don't know," said Mama hesitantly. "Ya'll will have to sleep in sleeping bags, and you're not going to sleep well on the floor.

Tomorrow's going to be a long day if you don't get enough sleep tonight. You'll be so much more comfortable in your own beds."

"Oh, we'll be fine!" we protested in unison.

"I sleep better on the floor," I stated, shaking my head vigorously.

"Yeah. We do, too," chorused my brother and sister. We all looked to our parents expectantly.

Daddy was the first to give in. "It's all right with me if it's all right with your Mama," he said.

Mama shook her head in exasperation, but relented. Mission accomplished!

After gathering on the couch so that Mama could read *The Night Before Christmas,* we rushed up the stairs. Sleeping bags and pillows came out of the linen closet and were laid on the floor side by side. With a kiss to each of us and lots of good nights, sleep tights and I love yous, we crawled into our sleeping bags. As soon as the door shut behind Mama and Daddy, Phase Two went into action.

My brother crept out of his sleeping bag and scooted over to his bed where the equipment was hidden underneath the mattress. Flashlights were passed out and checked over and over to see if they worked. The lights flickered on and off in the darkened room indicating that battery power was sufficient. He carefully stuffed the rope under his sleeping bag, and, just in case we accidentally fell asleep, my sister set the alarm clock, muffling it with her pillow. We giggled and whispered in the darkness, listening out for Mama and Daddy's footsteps and the clip-clop of reindeer hooves.

At some point, unbeknownst to any of us, we each drifted off to sleep. Then, sometime in the early morning hours, I was awakened by my brother. The soft glow of the moon filled his room with an eerie light. Shadows danced on the wall.

My brother whispered in a shaky voice, "I hear him! He's downstairs right now! Listen!"

I bolted upright in my sleeping bag, my ears peeled for any unusual noise. I shook my sister, and like my brother and I, she sat up, too. And that is when we heard it. We each heard the unmistakable sound of creaking floor-boards. Without a doubt, Santa's shiny black boots were traipsing around downstairs! The stout man with a snow-white beard was here in our house! Our keen ears even detected sounds on the roof. Reindeer, perhaps? I looked at my brother. He looked at my sister. A mixture of fear and excitement filled our trembling bodies.

"What are we going to do now?" asked my sister.

Suddenly, trapping Santa did not seem like such a good idea to any of us. After all, what would we do with him once we captured him? It would be terribly selfish to keep him to ourselves. Besides, what if he decided to take our goodies back to the North Pole? What if he never came to see us again? Without another word passing between us, the alarm was switched to the off position, and we each quickly crawled back into our sleeping bags and covered our heads. After all, we felt that we had indeed accomplished our overall mission. Without a doubt, Santa was real!

The rest of that very long night passed without incident, though we undoubtedly slept more fitfully. Finally, early morning arrived. All was quiet in the house, and the moon still shown in the sky. By now, however, we felt that it was safe to trek downstairs. It was still darker than it was light, so we pulled out our trusty flashlights and slowly opened the door. Thankfully, Mama and Daddy were fast asleep in their room. We tiptoed down the stairs to the living room and peeked around the corner nervously. Though no words passed between us, we were each still concerned that Santa knew about our little plan and, perhaps, had left switches and coal. But there before our eyes were goodies galore—boxes and packages, baskets of candy and fruit, and, best of all, brand-new bicycles! We could barely contain ourselves, but the early hour meant that we could not possibly wake up Mama and Daddy yet. We quietly tiptoed back up the stairs and plopped on the floor amidst the tangle of sleeping bags and pillows, whispering excitedly about what we had seen. Secretly, however, we were each relieved that Santa, with all of his infinite wisdom, had not caught us trying to catch him!

While Christmas Eve may have been the longest day of the year for my sister, brother and me, Christmas was always the shortest. When we could no longer stand the anticipation, we raced into my parents' bedroom and pounced on the bed, waking Mama and Daddy from their reverie. Led by our sleepy-eyed parents, we clamored down the stairs. Squeals of joy and excitement echoed throughout the house for hours.

Now, I have my own children who complain that Christmas Eve is much too long, and I have no doubt that they, too, have pondered the credibility of the Santa tales that they have heard. Perhaps they have plotted and planned like my siblings and I did, but I have a feeling that, like us, they will choose to let Santa perform his Christmas duties without interruption. Just in case, though, I think I will hide the flashlights and rope until after the holiday season.

Terri Duncan

7

INSIGHTS
AND LESSONS

Of two sisters, one is always the watcher, the other the dancer.

Louise Gluck

Pass It On

A true friend gives freely, advises justly, assists readily, adventures boldly, takes all patiently, defends courageously, and continues a friend unchangeable.

William Penn

My sister, Nancy, is probably the most generous person I know next to God himself. She lives and breathes sharing. Not a single soul comes within arms' reach of her generosity without walking away with their hands full of *something*—possibly a selection from her wholesale shop (an unused dining room chock-a-block full of giftware that she can wrap in a flash) or maybe a sample of homemade jam or salsa from her storehouse of canned goods.

At best, you could luck out and leave with a half-dozen homemade biscuits. And if you dawdle long enough in the driveway, she will soon be shoving a sack full of home-grown vegetables through the car window . . . just for you to take home and enjoy.

It is difficult to believe, then, that counting all the gifts my sister has given me in a lifetime, including those she hides in my suitcase when I am leaving town, I should so clearly remember the one she gave me back in the '60s when I was nothing but a selfish, spoiled and lazy little sister.

As a newlywed, I hated doing laundry. I didn't like sitting in a Laundromat . . . didn't like spending the money . . . didn't like spilling soap powder all over my car . . . and didn't like folding clothes. However, I loved going to my sister's house, where we could pass the day away sharing an intimate sister kind of fun.

So, at her suggestion, and with no resistance on my part, we arrived at an outstandingly simple solution to my resentment of having to keep the clothes clean. I would take all *my* laundry to *her* house. Together, we could sip on iced tea and munch on lunch, killing time while the dirty shirts and underwear swished around in her washing machine. It was a brilliant idea and one that I initiated immediately.

Weekly, I hauled several baskets full of dirty laundry through Nancy's front door and on into the kitchen near the washer and dryer. She would dive right in to the event, happy as a lark to be separating the darks from the lights. After she pushed the start button on the first load, we lost no time in resuming our visit.

As the day wore on, back and forth she went . . . dumping all my wet clothes into the dryer, reloading, folding the towels and stacking them neatly into the baskets. I stayed calm at the end of the kitchen table, perched with my Tupperware glass in hand, chattering a mile a minute as she took care of business. It did not occur to me to get up and offer any assistance; she looked so truly happy to be helping. Nor did I offer any favors in return for the wear and tear on the appliances. No, I just sat there, week after week, letting her jump up and down at the sound of every buzzer. In the afternoon (ready for a little nap after such a filling lunch), I would mosey out to the car, reload the trunk and head on home.

Well, they say all good things must come to an end, and in the autumn of the following year, my husband changed jobs, and we were off to Indiana. It was sad saying good-bye to my family . . . even more heartbreaking saying good-bye to "Laundry Day" at my sister's house. I don't know, maybe it was the guilt I was feeling on my last day there, suddenly realizing that she had never complained, never asked for reimbursement, never teased me into helping her . . . never did *anything* but be the loving, older sister she had always been to me.

We carried out the last basket of clean clothes and stood in the driveway. With our arms around each other in a final embrace, I stuttered out a thank-you for all she had done, an apology for having been such a bother. I asked if I could please pay her for all the soap, all the time and all the hot water I had used over the course of a year.

At this point, my dear sister responded by doing something I have seen her do a thousand times. Lovingly, she cupped my cheeks into the palms of her hands and looked me straight in the eye, pausing until she had my full attention. Then in her sweetest voice, she gave me one of the most precious gifts I have ever received.

"Promise me you will pass it on," she whispered. "There will be others who need a place to do their laundry. Promise me you will pass it on."

And her selfish, spoiled and lazy little sister whispered back, "I promise."

Charlotte A. Lanham

Lessons of the Heart (Pendant)

The best portion of a good man's life is his little, nameless, unremembered acts of kindness and of love.

William Wadsworth

Stolen. The word made me shudder just to think of it. I had only taken the necklace off because the clasp on the chain needed a little repair, and I thought I might lose it if I wore it that day. Not wanting to take the chance, I took it off and placed it carefully in my dresser drawer. That same day, our next-door neighbor burglarized our house, taking my pendant as well as other pieces of jewelry and money. It seemed destined that my cherished pendant would be lost to me.

It was not just any pendant; this was a gift given to me by my son for Mother's Day, a gift paid for with money he earned from his very first job. It was my most prized possession, and now it was gone.

"Hey, want to go shopping?" I picked up the phone to hear my sister's cheery voice. I hadn't planned on shopping. I was in the midst of a foul mood and didn't really

want to be saved from it. In fact, I was in the midst of trying to find a word for my curmudgeon-like behavior—
irascible, crabby, downright cranky, in a funk, in a snit. Ah!
That was it! I was in a snit and, oddly enough, enjoying
every miserable minute of it.

Usually, I'd jump at the chance to go shopping, especially with Mary Lou; usually, just hearing her voice
cheers me up. But, for the time being, there was a hole in
my heart, and I wasn't about to let anyone take away my
power to make myself miserable.

With some urging, although my mood had not improved
significantly, I reluctantly agreed to go. We were closing in
on Christmas, and shopping was on my to-do list.

Besides, talking to Mary Lou usually helps; she always
puts things into perspective. I just couldn't shake my feelings of anger and resentment toward the neighbor to
whom I had opened my house during his younger days,
since he was almost the same age as my son.

My sister and I had talked about it on a number of occasions; this was another sequel.

Still, Mary Lou listened sympathetically as I vented. The
only way to rid myself of the anger was to get a duplicate
of my heart pendant. Mary Lou worked her usual magic as
she verbally peeled away, layer by layer, the dark mood
that surrounded me. With the promise of checking some
jewelry stores, we shifted topics to Christmas, focusing on
gift ideas for our families; we even tackled our Christmas
dinner menu.

At the mall, we made a beeline to the nearest jewelry
store. The saleslady listened patiently, but I knew she was
too busy to hear all the details. I described the pendant
to her: a filigreed gold heart inset with garnets. She
explained that the stock of items changes over time, and
that I may never find the exact duplicate of my pendant.
Disappointment struck again, but I had to go on; it was

Christmas, and I had plenty of shopping to do for family and friends.

Mary Lou, supportive as always, patted my arm. "Don't worry," she whispered to me as we left the store. "We're not done yet."

That is her essence: never give up. This was not the first time that she bolstered my sagging spirits. Fifteen years earlier, I underwent two spinal-cord surgeries that rendered me paralyzed from the shoulders down. During my most troubled moments while undergoing physical therapy, Mary Lou was there for me. Each weekend while I was in the rehabilitation center, and even after my discharge home, she stayed with me, bringing my then-three-year-old nephew, Kenny, to play with my four-year-old son, Jeffrey.

At the same time, she researched the topic of motivational tapes and brought them for me to watch. This was the time to work and achieve, not to sit back and wallow in self-pity. That was her gift to me back then.

We finished our shopping trip, all the while checking all the jewelry stores we could find. The heart pendant could not be replaced. It was time to come to grips with that conclusion.

Several weeks later, on Christmas morning, my family and I fulfilled our traditions. We opened our gifts and spent time together before leaving on the hour-long drive to my sister's house in the northern part of the state.

At Mary Lou's house, our day is steeped in more traditions. We had breakfast together, and then we exchanged gifts. Mary Lou handed me a small, beautifully wrapped box. I looked at the box, and then at Mary Lou. Inside was a gold heart pendant enhanced with several rubies! It wasn't like the one I had lost, but even a duplicate wouldn't be the same as the one I had lost. I know that now. This one represented an attempt to heal a wound that had previously refused to close.

As we embraced, Mary Lou whispered, "See? I told you we weren't done yet!"

There were tears, more hugs and smiles, and a lesson learned: Sometimes it takes a painful event to teach us what is most important in life. It is impossible to replace anything we lose, whether it is family, friends, pets or a heart pendant. It is important to enjoy what we have while we have it. Anger only prevents us from enjoying the moment to the fullest.

My sister, Mary Lou, taught me that lesson. And on occasion when I forget, she's always there to provide the refresher course.

Beyond that, I learned that it is Mary Lou who has the heart of gold.

Donna Lowich

Turning Point

Many turning points in people's lives come as firsts. Right up from babyhood—first birthday, first tooth, first step, first word—in whichever order they come, and then as you grow—first grade . . . of course, who can forget the first crush, first date, first kiss, or first boy/girlfriend, either? But mine didn't come as a first . . . it was actually a fifth, the fifth time I had been made a big sister.

I was ten years old when my last little sister, Billie Raven Patty Mahan, was born. She was the last of eleven and an "oops" baby. Mom had had her tubes tied before Raven was conceived. Lucky for him, the doctor didn't get sued, and lucky for me, I got a best friend.

Mom was in the hospital quite a bit before Raven was born. Raven was a big, healthy baby (we all were), weighing nearly nine pounds. When my parents brought her home, she cried and fussed almost constantly. Dad said that was because they had given her a shot.

Her older siblings, including me, thought it was fascinating that she had four names, whereas some of us only had two. And other than the interest any new baby elicits in young children, the fact that she was the last of us only added more.

Still, I didn't like it much when I was given the task of babysitting. I had never really had that job before because I was too young, but now whenever Mom had work to do outside, I was on duty. Grudgingly, I danced Raven to sleep, played with her, soothed her when she cried. Somehow, along the way, I fell in love with that wriggling baby.

Of course, I have four other little sisters, but Raven and I share a special bond. Maybe it's because I was still just a child when she was born, and for several hours each day, she was my only playmate. We grew up together. When I let Raven fall off the bed too much and Dad told me I couldn't watch her anymore, I felt as though my whole world had fallen apart.

The turning point in my life was when I learned what being a big sister really means. It's not just sharing the same blood and happening to be older. It's being there as a friend and as a guiding light, entering into childish games and trying to set limits at the same time, sharing what you know about growing up so it's not quite as scary for them as it was for you.

It's not easy. But it could be the very meaning of the saying, "The most rewarding thing you will ever experience is being important in the life of a child."

For me, that is the definition.

I sort of got a taste of motherhood before I was ever old enough to have a baby of my own. I still lug Raven around on my hip, so I understand what it's like to feel more complete when a little head is tucked under your chin. She will be seven this November, and she still asks to be picked up sometimes, burying her face in my neck and hanging on until her world seems all right again. When her hand slips inside mine, I feel blessed and humbled. Even though I'm human, with all my faults and flaws, she loves and respects me.

I've learned a lot of lessons that I will carry with me when I become a mom. One is that it's always important to see things from the child's point of view because it's so much different from our own adult one—innocent and pure—and we can learn so much from it. I've learned that yelling only makes everything worse, but sometimes you have to . . . just not at the child. But most of all, I've learned to make special times together with each of my little sisters, to make silly little traditions to share, to tell them I love them as many times a day as possible and again just before they go to sleep, and to let loose and have fun on their terms. Largely, thanks to them, I was spared of going through the classic teen angst of not wanting to be related to my family, doing things just because everyone else is doing them, or hiding in a shell. And I learned what it's like to love someone so much it makes you cry.

Raven taught me that to hold your little best friend in your arms right against your heart is one of the best feelings in the world. When you're close enough to someone, you react to their touch, their voice, and even their smell, right in the middle of your heart. I think it has to do with pheromones and imprinting.

Turning points often steer people's lives irreversibly in a direction and even help them find their place in the world. Mine did both. Without children in your life, you can become self-centered and more concerned with yourself than others. When you're a mother or mother-in-training (like me), you focus on the little lives that depend on you and become a better person for it. When you spend as much time as I do with children, your view on life has a childish touch to it, so you notice things other people don't, and things about people that others don't. It makes you more sensitive to small things and to other people's feelings.

And, of course, it makes you very aware of how your

actions affect other people. You realize that you're an example to others. That can be awful scary all by itself, but it can also be a source of great pride and satisfaction.

No matter what I do or become, I've already got my first, and most important, degree: big sister for life. And I will always have it with me because it is written on my heart.

Penelope Mahan

Diamonds, Sisters and Mrs. Sperry

*It brings comfort to have companions in what-
ever happens.*

Saint John Chrysostom

Growing up, my sister, Shelby, and I never got along
very well. We argued about practically everything: whose
turn it was to empty the dishwasher, which television
show we would watch, why one of us needed to use the
bathroom first, how my blue sweater ended up in her
closet. We were sisters; we weren't really friends.

My senior year in high school, I found a job at a jewelry
store in the mall. By mid-November, they needed extra
help in the gift-wrapping department. I arranged an interview for Shelby, and she got the job.

Since she didn't have her driver's license yet, I became
her transportation. I was going to work anyway, so it
shouldn't have been that big a deal. But the dynamic of
two teenage sisters, who didn't get along very well in the
first place, all alone together in a car—something bad was
bound to happen.

It was Christmas Eve. I can't remember what sparked

our disagreement on this particular day, but Shelby and I left the house arguing. We bickered all the way to work. By the time we reached the mall, our verbal assaults turned physical. Lanky arms grabbed each other as we slapped and pushed in the bucket seats of my '71 Mercury Montego.

"You're such a dork," I yelled, as I pulled into a parking spot.

"I hate you," she retaliated.

My fingers grabbed a clump of her shiny blonde hair and pulled hard. Shelby started crying. Instead of consoling her, I took the opportunity to escape. Jumping out of the car, I slammed the door and rushed ahead of her through the mall and into the jewelry store.

Shelby arrived a few minutes later. Her face was puffy; her eyes red. Mascara left the telltale signs of our argument streaked across her cheeks.

Out of the corner of my eye, I saw Mrs. Sperry, the gift-ware and china salesperson, put an arm around my sister as they walked through the store.

Christmas carols played over the intercom while Shelby manned the gift-wrap station in the back. I stayed busy on the sales floor with last-minute gift-givers. I was so occupied with Christmas Eve shoppers that I quickly forgot about my sister and the fight.

The boss closed the doors at 5:00 P.M. sharp. We sales-people began the task of pulling merchandise from the display cases to lock away, safe in the vault. As usual, Mrs. Sperry joined me in the center jewelry bay.

Everyone else in the store was called by their first names, but we all addressed this nearly eighty-year-old woman as Mrs. Sperry. Soon, the two of us had pulled all the merchandise from the drawers. Pendants, gold chains, bracelets, earrings, pocketknives and watch fobs lay neatly in the trays.

I grabbed the first stack of trays to load in the vault. As I did, Mrs. Sperry's hand reached out for mine. Her perfectly manicured nails dug ever so slightly into my skin.

Setting down my load, I looked at her. Her pale blue eyes pierced mine.

"Did I ever tell you that I am an only child?" she whispered.

I looked at her hand that clenched mine so tightly and tried to get loose. She was a tiny woman, under five feet tall, but she had quite a grip for an elderly person.

"No," I answered, wondering where she was going with this announcement.

"My parents died decades ago, and my husband has been gone nearly twenty years," she continued. "What I wouldn't give to have had a sister to share life with." The sides of her mouth turned downward, but her message didn't penetrate my heart.

"We just don't get along," I complained. "Shelby is so annoying."

Mrs. Sperry's face turned stony as her nails dug deeper into my hand. "Then, learn to get along. If you don't, one day you will surely regret it."

The passion in her voice caught my attention. She loosened her grip, and we walked silently to the safe.

No packages were exchanged at the jewelry story that Christmas Eve, but Mrs. Sperry most certainly gave me a gift. It took someone who missed out on having a sister to remind me that sisterhood was truly a treasure.

On the way home, I apologized to Shelby, and she did the same. Our family went to Grandma's house that evening and ate Christmas Eve dinner, then opened presents.

I can't say that my sister and I've never had our differences in the last twenty years since we worked at the jewelry store, but I never forgot Mrs. Sperry's words of wisdom. Shelby and I have shared her happy marriage, my heartbreaking divorce, her devastating chronic disease, the trauma of our father's murder, and the blessings we both received from having children late in life.

Mrs. Sperry was right. The person who has been beside me most often in the joy and the sorrow was my sister, Shelby. That Christmas Eve in the jewelry store, I learned that sisterhood is a gift, more precious than jewels.

Stephanie Welcher Thompson

Seeing Is Believing

Faith is the substance of things hoped for, the evidence of things not seen.

Hebrews 11:1

The first time I saw her, I thought she was the most beautiful one-day-old baby in the world. My baby sister looked like the Gerber baby on the baby food jars, with pink rosebud lips, rosy cheeks and a perfectly shaped little head, which I held tenderly and carefully when my parents let me hold her.

As a ten-year-old, I was extremely proud Mother and Daddy chose my name for her: *Phyllis Anita Martin.* I adored *my* baby, helping Mother by bringing diapers, feeding Phyllis and even warming bottles of formula in the middle of the night. I waked each time Phyllis cried and ran to the kitchen to save Mother a few steps. She seemed so tired those days, and I stood in awe of the miracle that had happened to my mother's body as she had grown and prepared to give birth. I had just become a Christian that summer, and my life was filled with the excitement of new birth inside my heart as well as the new birth of a baby sister.

When she was one, Phyllis and I shared a room, where she remained until I married and moved to a home of my own. She was always my little girl and companion. Unlike my brother, who was close to my age—and constantly pulling my pigtails, punching my dolls' eyes out with a two-finger jab, or breaking their arms with a karate chop—Phyllis brought only joy into my life. She adored me, and the feeling was mutual.

I'll never forget the day when Phyllis, then two, pedaled her tricycle off the side of our front porch for a ten-foot fall down a rocky slope. Our whole family rushed her to the small hospital in our town. I cringed with every jab of the needle as I watched the doctor stitch up the gash in her forehead just above her eyebrow. She was so little and so terrified that I would have gladly taken her place—even though I was afraid of stitches and shots myself. Over the years, I was grateful that she didn't have to go to the hospital any other time.

As she grew into adolescence and adulthood, Phyllis and I remained close. Though we loved our brother, Jim, he didn't enjoy the same things we girls shared in special moments. I helped her shop, and grinned with pride at her piano recitals, basketball games and church activities. She became a wonderful young Christian leader in our church. She was only four feet, eleven inches tall and ninety-seven pounds, but she was a great Christian with a big heart.

Then came the days when Phyllis married and became pregnant with her own baby. On the day she went into labor, I stayed at home with my two small children, waiting for a call from my parents, who hovered near her at the regional hospital in a nearby town. Daddy called me midmorning.

"Edna, please pray. Phyllis is not doing well. The baby is big, and she's so small . . . and the doctor says she's going blind."

"What?" I said in disbelief. "Going blind! What causes that?"

"The doctor says it happens a lot during childbirth. Physical and mental trauma cause it."

I couldn't stay at home a minute longer. I got a baby-sitter and rushed to the hospital. I prayed all the way. Before I ran out the door, I picked up a book on prayer I'd been reading. It had suggested we thank God for answers to prayer even before we receive them. As I drove, my prayers ricocheted between positive expectancy and fearful begging: "Lord, thank you for already healing Phyllis. I know you're watching over her as the baby's being born—but, oh God, please don't let her be blind. Heal her eyes and her heart of any trauma. I know you're healing her right now, God, because you've promised that by your stripes we were healed—but I'm so afraid! Please, Lord. Don't let her die. Don't let her tear; don't let her go blind. I have faith that her baby will be as beautiful and healthy as *she* was when she was born—but, oh Lord, give the baby health and vigor and an easy birth. . . ." I stopped praying in the hospital parking lot and ran in. A nurse directed me upstairs, where Mother, Daddy and Ken, Phyllis's husband, stood outside her room with grave faces.

"The baby's here! It's a boy!" Daddy said.

"But she is blind. Can't see a thing," said Mother. Tears filled her eyes and overflowed onto her cheeks, and as I hugged her, she sobbed aloud on my shoulder. I cried, too. Daddy and Ken silently hugged Mother and me. Tears flowed.

Daddy explained that the doctor feared she'd lost touch with reality, slipping into a deep psychological state. His words paralyzed me. *No. Not my baby, Lord, not Phyllis.*

The nurse said I could go in. "Phyllis," I called from the door as I entered.

"Yes," she said, looking off in the distance. "I needed you. It's been hard." She searched the room with blank eyes. I reached out and held her hand.

"Oh, there you are," she said, looking slightly left of where I stood.

"You're my baby," I said, "and now, just think! You have a baby of your own." She searched for the glass of water sitting on the bedside table, fumbling, grasping.

"Here," I said. "It's over here." I helped her drink.

"Edna, did they tell you I'm blind? I wish I could see. I don't understand. . . . I'm scared."

I didn't know what to say. "Phyllis," I leaned over her bed, close to her face. "I believe God is healing you. I've been praying, thanking God that you are well. Your little boy is fine, and God has healed you!"

"Oh, Edna," she began.

I've said the wrong thing, I thought. *She's going to say, "Oh, Edna, don't start that God stuff with me. You don't understand. I'm blind. That's a fact."*

Instead, she said, "Oh, Edna . . . I can . . . see your face! I see you!"

She looked around the room. "And I can see the water glass . . . and the table! And, look! I can see the door . . . and even a dust bunny under that chair!"

She was right. There was a small ball of dust under the chair. "You can see!" I shouted, grinning widely. "Oh, Phyllis . . . you can see!"

"I'm so happy! The baby is wonderful. And I want to have another baby—maybe next year. . . ."

This was not the voice of a woman in trauma who couldn't bear to face childbirth. She was whole! Happy! Facing the future with courage! At the nurse's nod, I joined Mother, Daddy and Ken in the hall. This time we formed another circle as we hugged.

"She can see! God has healed her!" I said.

"Thank the Lord!" said Daddy.

"Amen. Amen," echoed Mother and Ken. Tears of joy flowed as we praised our Lord.

Edna Ellison

A Sister's Love

I stood there listening to the stern words of my father. He had gathered us into our enclosed patio and had the look on his face that told us all that one of us did something wrong.

"Which one of you did this?" he asked with a sharp voice. We all stared down at the floor containing the art of a child's handwriting in chalk. I suppose that had been a no-no for us, although I can't say I quite remember that part when I was committing this horrible crime.

I stood there, trembling on the inside and hoping that no one else could see it. *Will he know it was me?* I fretted. Too scared of the consequences of telling the truth, the only words that came from my mouth were, "Not me, Dad."

The others denied it as well. Of course, we knew that one of us must have done it, but I, being the youngest and smallest of the three, just couldn't find the courage to tell the truth.

It wasn't that I was a bad kid; lying was not normal behavior for me. But the look on my dad's face that evening sent a chill up and down my spine.

I couldn't bring myself to tell him the truth.

My dad had a way about him when I was a child that made me afraid of him. But I loved him for it, too, because it gave me limits and boundaries. I wanted to please him—so much, in fact, that I decided to hold back the truth that day. I couldn't let down the one man I looked up to.

Without saying a word, he disappeared for only minutes and came back with a piece of paper and a pencil. He was determined to find the culprit!

"I want each of you to write exactly what you see on the step," he ordered sternly.

I was not a stupid kid. When my turn came, I deliberately wrote the words differently. So when my dad compared the handwriting, he still couldn't tell which one of us did it.

Frustrated, he stood a step above us and peered down at his three small kids.

"I'm going to give you one more chance to confess," he admonished.

He continued to stand there for a few moments, but to me it seemed like an eternity. Not surprisingly, neither my brother nor my sister spoke up. Why should they? I was the one who had done it. *Should I say something? Was it too late?* Every time I almost got up the courage, I talked myself out of it. *He'll be mad!* So again, frightened, I held my tongue.

"Well, if someone would have come forward when I asked, there would have been no punishment."

Oh, no! I've lost my chance! Now it's too late. Stupid, stupid, stupid! I should have confessed! Now I'm gonna get it! I berated myself.

He took us all in the house as tears welled up in my eyes.

"Since none of you seem to have done it, then you all get a spanking," he declared.

Still, I stood there and said nothing. The last thing I wanted was a spanking! I didn't know what to do.

"I did it," someone said, and I was pretty sure it wasn't me.

I looked around to see my sister, Sue, come forward.

Huh? She did it? No, she didn't. I did! Why was she taking the blame for something I did?

Feeling guilty, yet still too scared to 'fess up, I stood there knowing my sister was going to get spanked for something I did. Perhaps if this were a Disney movie or a children's story, this is the scene or chapter where I would leap forward with my confession, preventing my sister from taking the heat for my actions. But this wasn't a movie or a fictional story. And I didn't have the courage. I let it happen. She got spanked because I didn't speak up.

My sister and I didn't talk about that day for many years. We were teenagers by then. Sitting around the living room, talking about days long past, I recalled out loud the time when this happened. Knowing that it was safe to tell my dad it was really me now that we were all older, I finally confessed. I remember Dad looking at me with wide eyes and a dropped mouth. "And you let your sister take the blame for you?" he asked, half-kidding. "I didn't spank her hard anyway." He laughed.

My sister, Sue, didn't seem surprised at all by my confession. Of course, she had always known it was either my brother or me. She wasn't upset with me. She simply kidded me about it and still does.

Sue was my protector, my worrywart and my best friend. She still is. That day, which now seems so long ago, she would have rather taken the pain herself than see me suffer. She would do anything for me. I'm glad to say that as I've grown up, I can say without hesitation that I would do the same for her.

Lynn M. Lombard

"Do you have just a plain happy birthday?
I don't want success to go to her head."

Someone to Care

A sister is both your mirror—and your opposite.

Elizabeth Fishel

Regret is a bitter pill, one whose aftertaste stayed with me for over forty years. It all began one evening in 1958 when my new boyfriend, Lee, and I lounged in the living room, listening to Johnny Mathis records while the rest of the family, except Dad, who was at work, enjoyed television in the den.

Lee and I, both juniors at James F. Byrnes High, had been dating only a few weeks, still getting to know one another.

"Psst."

My brow furrowed in irritation as I turned and peered at my ten-year-old sister, Patsy, hovering in the doorway. "What do you want, Patsy?"

She motioned for me to come outside the room, her face set in a strange way.

Frowning, I joined her in the hallway. She took my hand, tugged me to the kitchen and shut the door.

"What?" I asked impatiently as she turned to face me.

Then I noticed her red, swollen eyes.

"What's the matter?" I whispered, concerned. Patsy was not usually intrusive. She was, in fact, pretty thoughtful considering her age. I knew her propensity for mood swings now peaked in her adolescence. But even so, with my new beau waiting for me in the other room, I felt a bit annoyed. "What?" I insisted.

Her big blue eyes peered at me desperately, puddling anew with tears.

"Would you please ask Lee to drive you to get me some toothache medicine?" She snuffled and cupped her jaw with her hand. The strange set to her features, I realized, was pain.

"What a time for Daddy to be gone," I grumbled, aggravated because Daddy drove our only car to the mill. Patsy snuffled again. I thought, *She needs relief.*

Compassion kicked in. I nodded and turned to do her bidding.

Somewhere from the kitchen to the living room, my courage faltered. I looked at Lee, and the words stuck in my throat.

Coward! I berated myself, but still couldn't get the request out.

I had this thing—still do at times—about asking favors. And since, at that time, no Wal-Mart or 7-Eleven loomed on our rural horizon, the venture seemed mountainous. Lee and I were a fairly new item. *Would he mind?* In retrospect, I'm sure he'd have done it.

But in early 1958, such confidence eluded me. I glimpsed Patsy once more during the evening, peeking at me from beyond the door, desperation marking her young face. I tried again to speak the words only to have them gel in my throat. *Please let Patsy's pain disappear,* I prayed, knowing it was a cop-out.

A short time later, an aunt came to visit. Within minutes,

she'd whisked Patsy to a nearby friend's house to borrow some toothache drops to ease her misery.

Her generous spirit left me reeling with guilt. I felt every ounce the traitor I was. The why of my strange reticence evaded me.

Through the years that memory popped up sporadically, reminding me that no matter how sweet I thought myself, I was—on some level—actually a cold, unfeeling monster. With time's passage, the deed emerged as increasingly heartless.

Over time, I tried to make up that lapse to my sister. She, who baked cakes for her siblings on their birthdays while I couldn't even *remember* their birthdays, could outdo me in kindness with one hand tied behind her. No matter how hard I struggled to vindicate myself, that dark blot overshadowed all my efforts. And though the *why* finally revealed itself as adolescent insecurity, that was no excuse for failing my sister. I remained the mother of all hypocrites.

Recently, my phone rang. Patsy, now a Baptist minister's wife, invited me to visit their church for a special service. Since we often attend events there, I didn't think much about it until, during the service, Patsy stood to present an award to "Someone Special" in her life.

"Susie," she turned and smiled at me, "please stand."

On wobbly legs I rose, realizing she was about to honor me. *Me.* I cringed inside, horrified as, in her melodious voice, she began to speak.

"My sister, Susie, and I were always close. We slept spooned together, and she was always there for me, no matter what." Her smile grew and grew, and my heart sank lower and lower. "She was never unkind, like some older sisters I knew, but included me in what she was doing, let me hang around her friends. When our parents worked, she cared for me and our brothers. I always think of her that way—someone special whom God sent to care for me. I can't imagine life without my sis."

I felt like slithering through a crack in the floor as she went on to share other nice things about me and concluded with, "I'm so glad she hung in there with me through thick and thin. Thanks, Sis." The beautiful certificate she handed me felt weighted with cement.

I gaped at her through tears, wanting to shriek, *You've made a mistake! I don't deserve this!* I felt utterly despicable.

After the benediction, I pulled her aside and blurted, "Pat, I'm so sorry about that time, years ago, when I didn't take you to get toothache medicine." I waited, my heart tapping a bad dance, expecting that adoring look in her eyes to dull, then evaporate. Whoever said confession is good for the soul wasn't as mean as me.

Patsy gazed at me for a long moment. "When?"

I blinked, then began to breathe again. "You . . . really don't remember?"

"Nope."

But I did. "I'm sorry anyway." I grasped her fingers. "Please . . . forgive me?"

She squeezed my hand. "Okay." She chuckled, then shrugged. "But I don't remember it."

Wow. I felt like clicking my heels together, but knew I'd fall flat on my tush.

My day suddenly turned as sweet as the chocolate fudge my little sis and I used to make together during long ago holidays.

"Thanks, Patsy." I felt light and free and *wonderful. Forgiven.*

"For what?"

I threw my arm around her shoulder as we walked out together into the sun-filled day.

"For caring enough to forget."

Emily Sue Harvey

The Present

Two minds trading thoughts cause each mind to grow stronger.

Anna Lee Waldo

This past Christmas, my husband and brother-in-law gave my sister and me the same gift: a four-day trip with each other to a health spa. The fact that they got together without us knowing (we live 1,200 miles apart) and did something so extraordinary was quite amazing in itself; as a matter of fact, it could have sufficed as the gift because it was so out of the ordinary for both of them to do something like that. Earlier in the year our mother had passed away, and our husbands decided we needed time together to just, well, be together as sisters.

Needless to say, the experience, time, rest, relaxation, fellowship and, yes, even the exercising will not be easily forgotten. We were totally taken care of. For four days, we didn't do laundry, cook, grocery shop, carpool, wash dishes, clean bathrooms, make beds, walk dogs, run errands, and so on. For four days, we felt like the princesses we used to be in our make-believe world when we were young! For four days, we were young again, sharing secrets, laughing and crying, and even taking a nap or two. We didn't expect this gift. We didn't ask for it, didn't even really feel like we deserved it, but we accepted this present with tears of joy.

Choosing from a "menu" of services at the spa was half the fun as there were a multitude of facials, massages, personal training sessions, lectures, aerobics classes and more to pick from. It was a tough decision, but I managed to pick a handful of relaxing (as well as challenging) services that met my needs, while my sister picked her own. One of the things we both chose was an exfoliating body scrub. Each of us went to a private room where our skin was basically scrubbed and cleaned until all of the dead skin cells were gone and nothing remained but pure, cleansed, soft and renewed skin. I had never done anything like that before, and I thought I may as well take advantage of a total cleansing!

It was at that moment that I realized the real meaning behind taking advantage of this service that our husbands' Christmas gift had to offer. Both my sister and I needed a cleansing, but it was an emotional one. We needed this time to get rid of the pain, the hurt and the sorrow of losing our mother, and find the remaining pure, cleansed, soft and renewed relationship that we hold so dear as sisters. This was the present we received. We didn't expect it, didn't ask for it, didn't even really feel like we deserved it, but, oh, how we accepted the gift with tears of joy! To spend time as sisters was the gift of true love—the most perfect present.

Barbara Lundy

Elizabeth and Virginia

A sister is a little bit of childhood that can never be lost.

Marion C. Garretty

When my daughter and her husband found out they were expecting, it was quite a shock. They were already the proud parents of two girls who had just turned three and one!

"I don't need any more surprises," laughed my daughter as she headed off for her first sonogram. "I'm going to find out if it's a boy or a girl."

An hour or so later, I heard her coming in the back door and rushed into the kitchen to find out what my next grandchild would be. One look at her face told me something was up.

"Is everything all right?" I asked.

She nodded dumbly.

"Boy or girl?"

"Girl," she whispered and held up two shaky fingers. "TWO MORE girls."

I was laughing with relief, assuring her we'd all help

out, that four little girls under four (not to mention three under two) would be great fun.

There weren't so many multiple siblings then—certainly none on either side of our family—so everyone made a big fuss about it. We read everything we could get our hands on about twins and bought in duplicate. I soon realized that the only thing cuter than one baby dress is two baby dresses.

Carrying two babies while chasing after two toddlers made her pregnancy hard, but it was a healthy one. We all pitched in as promised, and soon there was a pretty nursery equipped with two of everything. A night nurse was hired in anticipation of those first few exhausting weeks at home. Our freezers bulged expectantly with nutritious casseroles. My granddaughters and their cousins and aunts and uncles looked forward to the arrival of the two little sisters. Still, my daughter couldn't quite get her mind around it. She had never really known any twins and finally admitted that the idea sort of "freaked her out." How would they relate to one another? What if one were better, smarter or prettier? What if they looked *exactly* alike? How strange!

Finally, the big day came. One month early, Elizabeth and Virginia were born, healthy and beautiful. They didn't look at all like either of their older sisters, but they did look like each other—exactly. They were identical in every way. In fact, the nurses warned us to keep some identifying mark such as a blue pin or a painted toenail on them once they were home and no longer wearing their Baby A and Baby B bracelets.

It was obvious that once my daughter saw her babies, she was totally in love, but I noticed a lingering flicker of concern in her eyes as she watched the tiny mirror images. We had all thanked the good Lord for a healthy delivery, but as I left the hospital that day, I added a prayer that something would erase the last little cloud of doubt my daughter was experiencing. I knew that soon enough the time would come when identical twin sisters would seem like the most normal thing in the world to her, but I was *her* mother, after all, and I thought that time needed to be sooner rather than later.

When I returned that evening, my daughter seemed completely at ease with the babies' "twinness," pointing out identical swirls of hair and shapes of ears and fingernails.

"Oh, by the way," she said, "the funniest thing happened right after you left today."

I picked up Virginia and she held Elizabeth as she recounted the tale.

"There are twin sisters who work as volunteers in the gift shop, and today is their eighty-fourth birthday. They asked if they could come up and see the babies and me. They were amazing—still look just alike and told me how great it has been being twins. It's wonderful how close they are." She smiled down at Elizabeth, remembering. "They were the neatest ladies," she said.

As I listened to her story, I wondered if it was coincidental or if my small prayer had indeed been heard and answered.

As if to erase any doubt, she added, "And Mom, their names are Elizabeth and Virginia."

Margaret Cunningham

My Sister, Myself

Both within the family and without, our sisters hold up our mirrors: our images of who we are and of who we can dare to be.

Elizabeth Fishel

I watch her as she crosses a busy street, step jaunty, head bent against a strong wind. I make a mental note to remind my sister that she really should cross streets more carefully in this traffic-choked town.

But as soon as we hug and sit down to talk, she'll dismiss that suggestion and move right on to the "agenda" she has: a list of the important subjects we must cover on this afternoon when we've both managed to stop the world for a sister coffee date. Talks about crossing streets can wait.

Ruthie is not just my big sister; she is my alter ego, my confidante, my mirror, my opposite, my counterpoint. I cannot imagine life without her—and she's been around from the instant I was born two years after she was, destined to forever disrupt her status as an adored only child.

She's long since forgiven me for so altering her life,

although my mother tells stories of the tortures she, the dispossessed older, inflicted on me, the usurper. And I surely remember the fierce fights we had as teenagers living in bedrooms next to one another when one of the oft-heard sounds was the banging of a door. "Stay out of here!" we would order one another furiously. Ten minutes later, we were giggling again.

As sisters, we never heeded Shakespeare's admonition of "Never a borrower or a lender be. . . ." What we had was community property. Every now and then, I'll still find something of Ruthie's—a scarf, a bracelet, a book—in a drawer or closet. It always reminds me that small pieces of our lives are in residence at one another's homes, and the idea pleases me.

Everyone says we're so different. And in so many ways, we are.

Ruthie is rational, analytical and altogether sensible. Her emotions don't rule her head. Small but mighty, she is also disciplined enough to eat a perfectly balanced diet— and to faithfully attend her aerobics classes and do her strength training.

I live in my nerve endings, eye the treadmill that leers at me and hang my jackets on it. My aerobics career lasted one week.

My sister is the family scholar, the sibling who read and read and read some more while I, the gadfly, partied. I wanted more of her academic diligence and determination. She wanted more of my social skills.

In midlife, we've borrowed from one another's stashes of strength, and we've happily shifted roles often and enthusiastically.

These days, my sister gives the best parties; I go to them—and then often stand in a corner marveling at my sister's ability to host disparate people so effortlessly.

Now I'm the passionate member of a book group, and

no matter how urgently I try to get Ruthie to join one, she hasn't. She's too busy having fun. . . .

Is something wrong with this picture?

We don't think so.

My sister and I have finally managed the feat that some unfortunate siblings never master: we've accepted one another as we are, and we've cast aside the labels that we thought might be glued to us forever.

It wasn't easy. It didn't happen overnight.

And believe me, there are still plenty of times when we drive each other crazy because, yes, we *are* different.

But Ruthie is the person who would walk barefoot across burning coals to help me. I'd do the same for her.

She is part of me, part of my journey through life, and the one person in the world with whom I shared both past and parents. We have our own language, a shorthand that I couldn't possibly explain to anyone else, and that often begins with the words, "Remember when?"

It's probably no coincidence that we "different" sisters have both ended up in the same career, that we are both writers who prefer the freelance life to a standard nine-to-five. It's also probably no coincidence that we share many of the same friends and most of the same values. And while we do not always share beliefs about politics and the state of the world, we do have remarkably similar laughs, voices and, yes, feet. We are blessed (or cursed) with high arches.

It doesn't matter to me that Ruthie, long divorced, fiercely independent, is far more unconventional than I am.

It doesn't matter to her that when we part from our precious coffee afternoons, I rush home to cook dinner while she dashes off to intriguing ethnic restaurants with her assortment of amazing friends.

What we share transcends those trifling differences.

Ruthie and I may squabble. We may even argue fiercely about the biggies, including the way to approach the challenges of our aging mother. But even if our styles, our habits and our basic personalities are astonishingly different—the ying and yang of siblinghood—we are joined at the soul.

Yes, sisterhood is powerful. And complicated. And rich.

And nobody knows that better than a woman who's lucky enough to be a sister.

Sally Friedman

"This is my sister. We're so close we would
have been twins if we could have arranged it!"

With Two Sets of Clothes

The time had come for Cathy to go off to university, and we were flat broke. Cathy had earned herself a partial scholarship, secured a job and even found a cheap apartment in exchange for helping out with the elderly landlady's laundry and errands. We were all proud, though I just didn't understand it. I mean, up until that point I don't think any of us Martin kids had actually willingly gone to school.

My brother, Ken, had to be led by the ear or chased by the stick if Mother caught him lollygagging. He would much rather be out rafting with his friend Donny or chasing gophers with his dog. My other sisters, Jeanette and Pat, enjoyed school strictly for the social vocation and tolerated the classes, if just for the chance to gossip and try on lipstick out of the watchful eye of Mother.

I myself found it quite a shock when told I was to go at the end of my last summer of freedom. I told my mother with all the stubbornness a five-year-old could muster that I would "try school for a while and see if I liked it." Before I made it a lifelong career and gave up my barefoot days, you see, I wanted to know if it would be worth it. But here was my sister, actually wanting to go voluntarily to school and (gasp) pay for it?

Cathy was going to university. Money was tight that year, I remember. We all wore hand-me-downs and castoffs, but this wouldn't do for such a fine institution. Mother, always the initiate, took in some barely worn but unfashionable suits from a neighbor and went to work on her sewing machine. We heard the rumble of the treadle machine as Mom worked through the nights after she had come home from work. Two skirts, two jackets, two blouses and a pair of trousers she set out to create from the suits and the rag bag. Thrift shops were scavenged as well as church sales, and my red silky top that Mother had deemed "too small" supplied the collar for a made-over blouse.

I cried and cried and cried some more. Now not only my sister was going away, but my favorite blouse as well! But when we saw Mother's handiwork, we gasped. Cathy was going to look "fashionable" even if the colors and fabric were a bit old-fashioned. She went with two "new" sets of clothes.

Life went on. Autumn frost gave way to frozen fields. Our pipes burst, and we had to gather snow from outside to melt on the woodstove for drinking water. Forget about using the inside facilities. I wondered if I could hold it till spring, or would I explode? Cathy probably had a nice, warm bathroom in Saskatoon. I imagined her in a fine house with lots of new friends. But when I finally got to visit, I was surprised to see the two tiny rooms she called "home." I tried to convince her to come back; I missed her, after all. But Cathy was determined to make it work.

Spring finally came, and the mud up past our shoes oozed in every crack in every wall in the basement. By summer the ruts were firmly dug in the road. There is a saying in the prairies, "Choose your rut carefully; you will be in it for a while." No one knew that quite like my sister.

Cathy was truly in for the long spell—four years of university in Saskatoon to learn to teach little kids like me. When she visited (which was seldom because 120 miles is a lot of gas money), she told us about the new and exciting things in her life—about books and people and places and how she lived. Her universe was expanding in leaps and bounds. Mine was still somewhere stuck in the mud. And yet she still wore those clothes Mom had made for her, day in and day out.

No one was more surprised than my family when I decided to return to school after dropping out to have my children. We would have to make sacrifices for Mom to get her dream of a "higher education." My brother and sisters and, yes, even my parents couldn't really understand why a thirty-something-year-old woman needed to pursue learning how to write well. No one understood, that is, except Cathy.

A week before my courses began, a box arrived from my big sister. In it were the two suits and blouses Mother had made for her. Cathy said in her letter, "They still have lots of wear left in them, and luckily they are in fashion again!"

"Choose your rut carefully," she wrote, "you may be in it for a while." So with nose to the grindstone, this little girl who thought she'd "try school and see if she liked it" returned to school, as before, dressed in her sister's hand-me-downs. But it doesn't seem to matter. I shall wear them proudly and never forget the "making do" and "alterations" that have to be made on the road to a better education.

Nancy Bennett

Best Friends and Sisters

For there is no friend like a sister, in calm or stormy weather, to cheer one on the tedious way, to fetch one if one goes astray, to lift one if one totters down, to strengthen whilst one stands.

Christina G. Rossetti

High-pitched voices lured me to the window. I pulled back the curtains and peeked through the blinds. On the sidewalk, my next-door neighbors, Samantha and Rebekah, rode bikes in the warm April sun. I watched as ten-year-old Samantha stood on one leg with the other slung over the seat of her blue mountain bike. From the edge of my driveway she waited for Rebekah, six, who was on a Big Wheel.

Once together, the girls rode the length of the next house. Samantha's bicycle went much faster than the tricycle Rebekah rode. Like before, Samantha waited for her sister to catch up. Then again, they started out together down the sidewalk toward the next house.

Playing with someone so much younger can't be fun for Samantha, I thought. *How can you go for a bike ride when one person is on a trike?*

Guilt churned in my stomach as I remembered another pair of girls—my sister and me.

I wasn't exactly *mean* to my sister, Shelby, even though she often said I was. It's just that it wasn't cool to play with her. Because she was two-and-a-half years younger, she wasn't as much fun as the kids my age. In fact, the only time I agreed to play with her was when there was no one else around. Doing things with Shelby was sort of a last resort.

"Wanna play?" she'd ask, her bright blue eyes hopeful.

"Naw, I'm busy," I'd reply, even if I was just lying in the chair watching television. She'd want to play A Barrel of Monkeys or Slap Jack—games I'd outgrown years ago. Looking back, I really don't know why I wouldn't give in to her more often. I remember how sad her eyes got and how the corners of her mouth turned down each time I said no.

I was in fifth grade and Shelby was in second grade when I started having friends spend the night. She'd knock on my door with her Shrinky Dinks. "Wanna play?"

Shelby prized her Shrinky Dinks and only brought them out on special occasions. I knew if she were offering to share, she really wanted to come in.

"Get out of here, you geek," I yelled. Shelby's bottom lip quivered as she slowly closed the door. We heard her sniff back her tears. But instead of feeling sad for her, my friend and I rolled on the ground giggling.

By the time Shelby was in fourth grade, she quit trying to play with me. I guess she gave up. I didn't think much about it at the time. I was just glad she stopped pestering me so much.

Eventually, Shelby found her own friends, a big group of them. They became really close—always at each other's houses or talking on the phone. It was like they were *her sisters* or something.

Like all kids, we grew up. Shelby and I went to different colleges, found jobs and got married. We didn't talk much and saw each other mostly on holidays.

But seeing how Samantha and Rebekah played together, I realized that not all sisters were like Shelby and me. Samantha seemed kind to her younger sister.

I walked out to get the mail. "Hi, girls," I called.

They waved from their driveway. Their mom sat on the porch. She waved, too.

I stepped across the lawn. We chatted about the weather and the daffodils that were pushing up through the dirt. The girls rode on down the sidewalk, Samantha first, then Rebekah.

"Your daughters seem to play together quite well," I remarked. "Watching them ride bikes, I noticed Samantha acted so patient with Rebekah."

"My daughters get along well most of the time," she confided. "Even though the girls possess different personalities and interests, I've taught them to appreciate each other."

Then she said something to me that I'll never forget.

"You have to treat your sister like your best friend. After all, your sister will be in your life longer than anyone else."

Walking home, I thought about her words. *Best friends with a sister?* I wasn't sure that Shelby and I were even friends at all. How I wish someone would have shared that idea with me when I was young.

My sister and I may have wasted thirty-five years on not being friends, but we still had a good thirty-five left. I went to the telephone and punched in the numbers.

Shelby answered.

"Wanna play?" I asked.

Stephanie Welcher Thompson

More Chicken Soup?

Many of the stories and poems you have read in this book were submitted by readers like you who had read earlier *Chicken Soup for the Soul* books. We publish many *Chicken Soup for the Soul* books every year. We invite you to contribute a story to one of these future volumes.

Stories may be up to twelve-hundred words and must uplift or inspire. You may submit an original piece, something you have read or your favorite quotation on your refrigerator door.

To obtain a copy of our submission guidelines and a listing of upcoming *Chicken Soup* books, please write, fax or check our Web site.

Please send your submissions to:

Chicken Soup for the Soul
P.O. Box 30880, Santa Barbara, CA 93130
Fax: 805-563-2945
Web site: *www.chickensoup.com*

We will be sure that both you and the author are credited for your submission.

For information about speaking engagements, other books, audiotapes, workshops and training programs, please contact any of our authors directly.

Supporting Others

With each *Chicken Soup for the Soul* book we publish, we designate one or more charities to receive a portion of the profits. A portion of the proceeds from *Chicken Soup for the Sister's Soul 2* will be donated to Camp to Belong.

Since 1995, Camp to Belong has been actively reuniting brothers and sisters placed in separate foster homes through mentoring, advocacy and summer camp programs. Lynn Price, founder, and her sister, Andi Andree, spent the majority of their childhoods living in separate homes. They didn't become friends, let alone sisters, until they became adults.

Over 900 separated siblings have been reunited, and Camp to Belong's programs are receiving both national and international recognition, including from Oprah Winfrey's Angel Network Use Your Life Award and the President's Service Award from The White House.

Camp to Belong is a year-round, national, nonprofit all-volunteer organization dedicated to reuniting brothers and sisters placed in separate foster homes for events of fun, emotional empowerment and sibling connection. They serve as emissary, intermediary and champion for the rights of siblings in foster care.

Camp to Belong strives to educate the nation about the plight of these resilient children and the importance of keeping siblings together in foster care or adoption, whenever possible. If separated, they encourage ongoing communication to insure a sense of belonging. They inspire them to higher education and a successful adult life through their events, care and support. Camp to Belong is not about finding a brother or sister. It is about reuniting siblings who may live in the same town, maybe even go to the same school. They may not have the opportunity to read bedtime stories together at night, wake up in the morning and have breakfast, argue about who is going to sit in the front seat of the car, attend school functions and sports activities together and share precious holidays.

Camp to Belong
9445 Sandhill Place
Highland Ranch, CO 80126
Phone: 888-7-BELONG

Who Is Jack Canfield?

Jack Canfield is the cocreator and editor of the *Chicken Soup for the Soul* series, which *Time* magazine has called "the publishing phenomenon of the decade." The series now has 105 titles with over 100 million copies in print in forty-one languages. Jack is also the coauthor of eight other bestselling books, including *The Success Principles: How to Get from Where You Are to Where You Want to Be, Dare to Win, The Aladdin Factor, You've Got to Read This Book,* and *The Power of Focus: How to Hit Your Business, Personal and Financial Targets with Absolute Certainty.*

Jack has recently developed a telephone coaching program and an online coaching program based on his most recent book, *The Success Principles.* He also offers a seven-day Breakthrough to Success seminar every summer, which attracts 400 people from fifteen countries around the world.

Jack is the CEO of Chicken Soup for the Soul Enterprises and the Canfield Training Group in Santa Barbara, California, and founder of the Foundation for Self-Esteem in Culver City, California. He has conducted intensive personal and professional development seminars on the principles of success for over 900,000 people in twenty-one countries around the world. He has spoken to hundreds of thousands of others at numerous conferences and conventions and has been seen by millions of viewers on national television shows such as *The Today Show, Fox and Friends, Inside Edition, Hard Copy,* CNN's *Talk Back Live, 20/20, Eye to Eye,* and the *NBC Nightly News* and the *CBS Evening News.*

Jack is the recipient of many awards and honors, including three honorary doctorates and a Guinness World Records Certificate for having seven *Chicken Soup for the Soul* books appearing on the *New York Times* bestseller list on May 24, 1998.

To write to Jack or for inquiries about Jack as a speaker, his coaching programs or his seminars, use the following contact information:

Jack Canfield
The Canfield Companies
P.O. Box 30880
Santa Barbara, CA 93130
Phone: 805-563-2935 • Fax: 805-563-2945
E-mail: *info@jackcanfield.com*
Web site: *www.jackcanfield.com*

Who Is Mark Victor Hansen?

In the area of human potential, no one is more respected than Mark Victor Hansen. For more than thirty years, Mark has focused solely on helping people from all walks of life reshape their personal vision of what's possible. His powerful messages of possibility, opportunity and action have created powerful change in thousands of organizations and millions of individuals worldwide.

He is a sought-after keynote speaker, bestselling author and marketing maven. Mark's credentials include a lifetime of entrepreneurial success and an extensive academic background. He is a prolific writer with many bestselling books, such as *The One Minute Millionaire, The Power of Focus, The Aladdin Factor* and *Dare to Win,* in addition to the *Chicken Soup for the Soul* series. Mark has made a profound influence through his library of audios, videos and articles in the areas of big thinking, sales achievement, wealth building, publishing success, and personal and professional development.

Mark is the founder of the MEGA Seminar Series. MEGA Book Marketing University and Building Your MEGA Speaking Empire are annual conferences where Mark coaches and teaches new and aspiring authors, speakers and experts on building lucrative publishing and speaking careers. Other MEGA events include MEGA Marketing Magic and My MEGA Life.

He has appeared on television (*Oprah,* CNN and *The Today Show*), in print (*Time, U.S. News & World Report, USA Today, New York Times* and *Entrepreneur*) and on countless radio interviews, assuring our planet's people that "you can easily create the life you deserve."

As a philanthropist and humanitarian, Mark works tirelessly for organizations such as Habitat for Humanity, American Red Cross, March of Dimes, Childhelp USA and many others. He is the recipient of numerous awards that honor his entrepreneurial spirit, philanthropic heart and business acumen. He is a lifetime member of the Horatio Alger Association of Distinguished Americans, an organization that honored Mark with the prestigious Horatio Alger Award for his extraordinary life achievements.

Mark Victor Hansen is an enthusiastic crusader of what's possible and is driven to make the world a better place.

Mark Victor Hansen & Associates, Inc.
P.O. Box 7665
Newport Beach, CA 92658
Phone: 949-764-2640 • Fax: 949-722-6912
Web site: *www.markvictorhansen.com*

Who Is Patty Aubery?

As the president of Chicken Soup for the Soul Enterprises and a #1 *New York Times* bestselling coauthor, Patty Aubery knows what it's like to juggle work, family and social obligations—along with the responsibility of developing and marketing the more than 80 million *Chicken Soup* books and licensed goods worldwide.

She knows because she's been with Jack Canfield's organization since the early days—before *Chicken Soup* took the country by storm. Jack was still telling these heartwarming stories then, in his training programs, workshops and keynote presentations, and it was Patty who directed the labor of love that went into compiling and editing the original 101 *Chicken Soup* stories. Later, she supported the daunting marketing effort and steadfast optimism required to bring it to millions of readers worldwide.

Today, Patty is the mother of two active boys—J. T. and Chandler— exemplifying that special combination of commitment, organization and life balance all working women want to have. She's been known to finish at the gym by 6:00 A.M., guest-host a radio show at 6:30, catch a flight by 9:00 to close a deal—and be back in time for soccer with the kids. But perhaps the most notable accolade for this special working woman is the admiration and love her friends, family, staff and peers hold for her.

Of her part in the *Chicken Soup* family, Patty says, "I'm always encouraged, amazed and humbled by the storytellers I meet when working on any *Chicken Soup* book, but by far the most poignant have been those stories of women in the working world, overcoming incredible odds and—in the face of all challenges—excelling as only women could do."

Patty is also the coauthor of several other bestselling titles: *Chicken Soup for the Christian Soul, Christian Family Soul* and *Christian Woman's Soul, Chicken Soup for the Expectant Mother's Soul, Chicken Soup for the Sister's Soul* and *Chicken Soup for the Surviving Soul.*

She is married to a successful international entrepreneur, Jeff Aubery, and together with J. T. and Chandler, they make their home in Santa Barbara, California. Patty can be reached at:

Self-Esteem Seminars
P.O. Box 30880
Santa Barbara, CA 93130
Phone: 805-563-2935
Fax: 805-563-2945

Who Is Kelly Mitchell Zimmerman?

Kelly Mitchell Zimmerman is currently a physical education teacher and has been a volunteer reader for the *Chicken Soup* series since the inception of the first book. Kelly was honored when her sister, Patty Aubery, president of Chicken Soup for the Soul Enterprises, suggested they collaborate on *Chicken Soup for the Sister's Soul 2*. Kelly currently resides in Southern California along with her husband, Chris, and son, Cody.

Kelly can be reached through the *Chicken Soup for the Soul* offices at 805-863-2935.

Contributors

Several of the stories in this book were taken from previously published sources, such as books, magazines and newspapers. These sources are acknowledged in the permissions section. If you would like to contact any of the contributors for information about their writing or would like to invite them to speak in your community, look for their contact information included in their biographies.

The remainder of the stories were submitted by readers of our previous *Chicken Soup for the Soul* books who responded to our requests for stories. We have also included information about them.

Becky Alban lives in Minnesota with her husband and daughter. Becky is a Sunday school teacher and works with children at her local elementary school. She enjoys reading, writing, sewing and crafting. You can reach Becky at *beckster@pro-ns.net.*

Wildlife artist **Nancy J. Bailey** is the author of *Clifford of Drummond Island*, the true story of her rascally Morgan horse, and its sequel, *Return to Manitou*. She lives in Michigan with her horses, dogs and cats. She still spends lots of time with her little sister, Amanda.

Glenda Barbre developed a love for writing while still a child in the Mt. Hood National Forest. As her life unfolded, she began writing for devotional books, among them *Ripples of Joy* and *All Is Calm, All Is Bright*, compiled by Cheryl Kirkling. Her work has appeared in *Guideposts, Angels on Earth* and *Reminisce*.

Nancy Bennett is gray haired, bespeckled and freckled—all part of her aging charm. She is currently involved in searching out her family roots. She is an essayist and historical writer who lives with her family and other animals on Vancouver Island. She has over 300 publications to her credit.

Melissa M. Blanco graduated from Gonzaga University in 1996. She was recently published in *Chicken Soup for the Mother of Preschooler's Soul*. She and her husband, Chris, reside in Bonney Lake, Washington, with their children, Madison and Peyton. This story is dedicated to Kaileen and Mary and all those who have grieved the loss of a child due to miscarriage.

Arthur Bowler, a U.S./Swiss citizen and graduate of Harvard Divinity School, is a writer and speaker in English and German. His work has appeared in several best-selling anthologies and in a bestseller in Switzerland. Look for his book, *A Prayer and a Swear*. Visit his Web site at *www.arthurbowler.ch.*

Cynthia Briggs celebrates her love of cooking and writing through her nostalgic cookbook, *Pork Chops & Applesauce: A Collection of Recipes and Reflections*. She enjoys writing book reviews and food columns; her newest endeavors include publishing a series of cook-booklets and writing children's books. Contact Cynthia through her Web site at *www.porkchopsandapplesauce.net.*

Lana Brookman lives in a small town in central Wisconsin. She teaches communication courses at the area technical college and instructs at-risk youth for an area school district. In her spare time, she enjoys spending time with family and friends, reading, writing and playing on her computer.

Renie Burghardt is a freelance writer who was born in Hungary. She has been published in many anthologies and magazines, including *Chicken Soup for the Christian Family Soul, Horse Lover's Soul, Grandma's Soul, Father and Daughter Soul* and *Cat Lover's Soul*. She lives in beautiful, rural Doniphan, Missouri. Contact her at *renie_burghardt@yahoo.com*.

Martha Campbell is a graduate of Washington University of St. Louis School of Fine Arts and a former writer/designer for Hallmark Cards. She has been a freelance cartoonist and book illustrator since 1973. She can be reached at P.O. Box 2538, Harrison, AR 72602 or at 870-741-5323 or *marthaf@alltel.net*.

Helen Colella is a freelance writer from Colorado. She has published educational books, fiction and nonfiction articles, and stories for both adults and children—several in *Chicken Soup* books. Assist Write Consultant services offers editing, book layout and story development. E-mail her at *helencolella@comcast.net*.

Barbara Andree Croce was born and raised in Belgium. Currently a fitness trainer, she has raised a family of three children in the United States with her husband and best friend, Rich. She loves to teach God's word to women internationally. You can e-mail her at *bcroce@verizon.net*.

Margaret Cunningham lives on Alabama's beautiful gulf coast with her husband, Tom. Her short stories have placed in several national contests, appeared in *Beginnings* magazine, the anthologies, *Hello, Good-Bye* and *Gardening at a Deeper Level*, and *Chicken Soup for the Dog Lover's Soul*. Please e-mail her at *peggymob@aol.com*.

Bonnie Walsh Davidson, M.Ed., of Marion, Massachusetts, is the author of *Breast Friends*. Davidson has turned her breast cancer experience into an avocation, publishing numerous pieces on breast cancer in several national magazines, as well as *Chicken Soup for Every Mom's Soul*. Her husband, Paul, encouraged her to spread her wings with a Web site, *PinkRibbon.com*, in the hopes of assisting other women diagnosed with breast cancer. Davidson is a mother of three and a full-time real estate associate for Jack Conway & Company, Inc., in Mattapoisett, Massachusetts, and chairperson of the Relay for Life in her community.

Cheryl Ann Dudley received a master's degree in English from the University of Idaho in 2004. She writes for the *Appaloosa Journal* in Moscow, Idaho, and enjoys riding her horses, hiking, playing tennis, reading and writing. She is working on her first book, which will be published in early 2007. Please e-mail her at *cheryldudley@moscow.com*.

Terri Duncan received her bachelor's, master's and specialist degrees from Augusta State University. She is an instructional technology specialist in Evans, Georgia, and is also a devoted wife and the mother of two delightful teenagers. Terri enjoys spending time with her family, reading and, of course, writing!

Dena J. Dyer is a wife, mom, writer and speaker from Texas. She loves to encourage women to find their hope, rest and joy in Jesus—our only true source of peace in the midst of a chaotic world. Her books include *Grace for the Race: Meditations for Busy Moms, The Groovy Chicks' Roadtrip to Peace* and *The Groovy Chicks' Roadtrip to Love*. Visit her Web site at *www.denadyer.com*.

Vivian Eisenecher holds a degree in business administration (magna cum laude), and a certificate in gerontology. Her previous published works have appeared in *Chicken Soup for the Single's Soul, Woman's World* and *Viewpoint.* Vivian enjoys walking, reading, writing and traveling. She resides in San Diego, California, and can be contacted at *vive@san.rr.com.*

Edna Ellison, Ph.D., international humorist/speaker/writer, has been featured with Focus on the Family. Author of many magazine articles and books, including the *Friend to Friend* series (Philippians, Ephesians, Hebrews), she loves serving as keynote speaker at Christian women's conferences, autograph parties and retreats. Contact her at *ednaE9@aol.com; www.ednaellison.com;* 864-579-3328.

Lizann Flatt is a writer and full-time mom to one son and two daughters in Ontario, Canada. It is her goal to help her own two daughters to grow up to enjoy the strong bond of sisterhood. Lizann enjoys reading, hiking, writing, and spending time with her husband and family, and now, much to her chagrin, wishes she could enjoy an acre of asparagus with them.

Tessa Floehr is a former science teacher now devoting her time to raising her two daughters. She enjoys writing, teaching crafts to children and teaching Sunday school with her husband. She and her sister are dedicated Bon Jovi fans who enjoy seeing the band live whenever possible. Contact her at *tessa@floehr.com.*

Peggy Frezon is a freelance writer and frequent contributor to *Guideposts, Sweet 16* and *Positive Thinking* magazines. She spends her free time watching her son Andy's baseball and basketball games, talking to her daughter, Kate, on the cell, and playing with her dogs, Kelly and Hudson. Please e-mail her at *ecritMeg@nycap.rr.com.*

For over three decades, **Sally Friedman** has been sharing her life with readers of national, regional and local publications. Her weekly column still apppears in her hometown newspaper in New Jersey. Many of her essays have appeared in the *Chicken Soup for the Soul* series. E-mail her at *pinegander@aol.com.*

Nancy B. Gibbs is a pastor's wife, a mother and a grandmother. She is an author, newspaper columnist and motivational speaker. Nancy has been published in numerous *Chicken Soup for the Soul* titles and other anthologies and magazines. For speaking engagements, please contact her at *Daiseydood@aol.com* or through her Web site at *Nancybgibbs.com.*

Janet Hall is the author of four previous stories in the *Chicken Soup for the Soul* series. She is also a playwright and an actress and loves to spend her free time traveling. You can e-mail her at *actingjanet@hotmail.com.*

Speaker-artist **Bonnie Compton Hanson** is the author of several books for adults and children, including the popular *Ponytail Girls* series, plus hundreds of published articles and poems. She also mentors new writers and leads writing seminars. Write to her at 3330 S. Lowell St., Santa Ana, CA 92707; call 714-741-7824 or e-mail *bonnieh1@worldnet.att.net.*

Patrick Hardin's cartoons appear in a variety of books and periodicals in the United States and abroad. He may be reached at 810-234-7452.

Emily Sue Harvey has published over twenty-five short stories, which appear in *Chicken Soup, Chocolate for Women, A Father's Heart, Whispering in God's Ear, Woman's Day, True Story, Compassionate Friends* and *From Eulogy to Joy.* Also known as Suzanne Miller, she is the author of *Homefires* and *Unto These Hills,* Southern mainstream novels. E-mail her at *Emilysue1@aol.com.*

Jonny Hawkins dedicates his cartoons in this book to his three sisters—Lisa, Becky and Ronelle. Over the last twenty years, thousands of his cartoons have appeared in *Women's World, Reader's Digest, Leadership, Forbes* and many other places. He has three calendars out—*Medical Cartoon-a-Day, Fishing Cartoon-a-Day* and *Cartoons for Teachers*—in addition to several books. He can be reached at *jonnyhawkins2nz@yahoo.com*.

Libby Hempen is married to her wonderful husband, Bob, and is Mom to Sam and Luke. She spends her time reading, traveling and doing anything outdoors. Currently, she is working on a gift book for fathers and more short stories.

Pamela Hackett Hobson is the proud mother of two terrific sons. Pam's first novel, *The Bronxville Book Club*, was featured in the *New York Times* article, "Buzzzz, Murmurs Follow Novel." The sequel is entitled, *The Silent Auction*. To find out more about Pam, visit *www.pamelahobson.com* or e-mail her at *author@pamelahobson.com*.

Louise Tucker Jones is an award-winning author and inspirational speaker. She is the author/coauthor of three books and holds a master's degree in creative writing. Her work has been featured in various magazines, including *Guideposts* and several *Chicken Soup* titles. Louise resides in Edmond, Oklahoma, and can be reached at *LouiseTJ@cox.net*.

Kevin Gerard Kilpatrick, writing under the pseudonym Kevin Gerard, recently signed a publishing contract with Emerald Falcon Press. The first book in the *Conor and the Crossworlds* series, *Breaking the Barrier*, should be available for purchase in the fall of 2006. Check the author's Web site for more information at *www. conorandthecrossworlds.com*.

Charisse J. Broderick King lives in Colorado with her husband and two young daughters, whom she is currently staying at home to raise. She received her degree in journalism from the University of Colorado. When she returns to the work-a-day world, Charisse hopes to work in development in the non-profit arena.

Angie Klink authored the lift-the-flap children's book, *Purdue Pete Finds His Hammer*. Her column, "From Testosterone Trenches," is about her two boys. She is published in *Our Fathers Who Art in Heaven* and several newspapers. She has won twenty-two American Advertising Federation ADDY Awards for copywriting. Visit *www. angieklink.com* or *www.mascotsforkids.com*.

Nancy Julien Kopp's writing reflects both her growing-up years in Chicago and many years of living in the Flint Hills of Kansas. She has published stories, articles, essays and children's stories in magazines, newspapers, online and in anthologies, including *Chicken Soup for the Father and Daughter Soul*. She is a former teacher who continues to teach via the written word.

Dolores Kozielski is a certified feng shui consultant trained in Kabbalah, Qigong, Tai Chi and I Ching. She is a professional author, published by major publishing houses, including HarperCollins and Scholastic. Dolores is also a contributor to *Chicken Soup Healthy Living Series/Stress*. She can be reached at *www.FengShuiWrite.com*.

Margie Lang is a published author of thirteen stories, nine in *Chicken Soup for the Soul* books. She is a Christian speaker at women's and children's groups in America and an English teacher to orphans with Serving Our World in Thailand and also in the Thai public schools. She has two granddaughters.

Charlotte A. Lanham lives in Duncanville, Texas, with her husband, Ray. She is a former columnist and a frequent contributor to *Chicken Soup for the Soul* books. She is also the cofounder of Abbi's Room, a nonprofit organization that provides beds and bedding for children of Habitat for Humanity families. E-mail her at *charlotte.lanham@sbcglobal.net.*

Lynn M. Lombard has been writing since she was a young girl. She has had two stories published in *Heartwarmers of Love,* a book of inspirational stories. She has also been published in several magazines. She is currently hard at work on her first novel.

Patricia Lorenz is an art-of-living speaker and writer and the author of six books, including *True Pilot Stories.* She's one of the top contributors to the *Chicken Soup* books with stories in twenty-seven of them so far. To inquire about having Patricia speak to your group, e-mail her at *patricialorenz@juno.com* or visit her Web site at *www.PatriciaLorenz.com.*

Donna Lowich works as an information specialist, providing information to people affected by paralysis. She enjoys writing about her family and personal experiences. Other hobbies include reading and counted cross-stitch. She lives with her husband and son in New Jersey. Her e-mail is *DonnaLowich@aol.com.*

Barbara Lundy received her degree from Columbia College, Columbia, Missouri, in 1974 and currently works as a writer for Calvary Chapel in Fort Lauderdale. Other than her time alone with God, Barbara's most precious time is with her husband and four children, when they are all home at the same time!

Catherine Madera is a freelance writer living in the Pacific Northwest. She has published in equestrian magazines and anthologies and is a contributing writer for *Guideposts.* She enjoys the country life with her husband, Mark, two children and a menagerie of animals. You can reach her at *maderam@wwdb.org.*

Penelope Mahan lives in Edmonton, Alberta, and is working on her first novel. She enjoys meeting youth, photography, camping and hanging out with friends. She loves hearing from her readers at *lilgully@yahoo.com.*

Rene Manley is a writer and counselor in Salem, Oregon. A nationally certified counselor, she works with children and writes about children and families. The author of a weekly newspaper column, *Friend of the Family,* she also writes fiction and educational curricula, as well as freelance/contract editorial work. Contact her at *renemanley@comcast.net.*

Jennifer Martin is a retired educator and television host/producer who, in her current evolution, is an author, speaker and metaphysics teacher living in northern California. She is the author of the novel, *The Huna Warrior: The Magic Begins,* and invites you to visit her Web site at *www.hunawarrior.com.*

Sharon McElroy is the second-born daughter of five girls. She is also a mother of three children—two sons and a daughter—and a proud grammy of three grandsons who educate her to the fullest. A debt-management advisor by day and a writer by night, Sharon hopes to share more stories and to have books of love poems published.

Recently published in *Birds & Blooms,* **Joan McKee** attends a writer's workshop conducted by Evelyn Minshull at the Senior Center in Hermitage, Pennsylvania. She has three sisters and one brother. This article is about her youngest sister, Janet. Joan is the mother of three children.

Dahlynn McKowen is one of *Chicken Soup for the Soul*'s most trusted coauthors, having created many titles, including *Chicken Soup for the Entrepreneur's Soul*. Dahlynn and her husband, Ken, are owners of Publishing Syndicate, an on-line business that offers writing and publishing tips. Sign up for their free e-newsletter at *www.PublishingSyndicate.com*.

Risa Nye is a San Francisco Bay Area writer and college counselor. Her essays and articles have been published in several local magazines and newspapers, which delights her no end. She has written a journal for college-bound students called *Road Scholar*, published by No Flak Press.

Stephanie Piro lives in New Hampshire with her husband, daughter and three cats. She is one of King Features' team of women cartoonists, "Six Chix." (She is the Saturday chick!) Her single panel, "Fair Game," appears in newspapers and on her Web site at *www.stephaniepiro.com*. She also designs gift items for her company Strip T's. Contact her at *piro@worldpath.net* or by mail at P.O. Box 605, Farmington, NH 03835.

Phyllis Ring coordinated a variety of programs on healing and spirituality for a Baha'i conference center and has published articles on health, spirituality and family in *Mamm*, *Christian Science Monitor*, *Bay Area Parent*, *SageWoman* and *Delicious Living* magazines. More information about her work is available at *www.phyllisring.com*.

Meredith Lawrence Robnett lives in Plano, Texas, where she continues to be an advocate for the prevention of AIDS in memory of her beloved sister.

Sallie A. Rodman's stories have appeared in various *Chicken Soup* anthologies, including *Recovering Soul, Mother and Daughter Soul, Healthy Living Series—Heart Disease* and *Stress*, numerous newspapers and magazines. She lives in Los Alamitos with her husband. Sallie writes to share the wonders of daily life with others. E-mail her at *sa.rodman@verizon.net*.

Ruth Rotkowitz is a freelance writer and English teacher. She has taught at both the high school and college levels and has published poetry and nonfiction articles in several publications. She is currently at work on a novel. She can be reached at *mideb@aol.com*.

Harriet May Savitz is an award-winning author of reissued groundbreaking books about the disabled, among them, *Run, Don't Walk*, which was turned into an ABC afterschool special produced by Henry Winkler. Other books include, *Hello, Grandparents! Wherever You Are* and *More Than Ever—A View from My 70s*. Visit her Web site at *www.harrietmaysavitz.com*.

Shelley Stolaroff Segal is a writer, composer and performer living in Greensboro, North Carolina. After earning a degree in English literature at UNC Chapel Hill, she received her theatrical training at the Drama Studio/London. Her latest work was recently published in the anthology, *Voices from the Spectrum*. She may be reached at *shelleys@iquest.net*.

Dayle Allen Shockley is the author of three books and hundreds of articles. She has been a special contributor to *The Dallas Morning News* since 1999 and offers editorial services through her Web site at *www.dayleshockley.com*. Write to Dayle at *dayle@dayleshockley.com*.

Susan Siersma values most time spent with family. Besides writing, organic gardening and reading, Susan enjoys (hopelessly trying to learn) playing the violin. Nature and the people around her are the inspiration for Susan's writing. She hopes her stories leave readers with a smile. You can reach Susan at *ssiersma@comcast.net.*

Joyce Stark lives in northeast Scotland and works in Community Mental Health. She is also a freelance writer, currently working on an adventure series to introduce younger children to elementary Spanish. She spends as much of her time as she can exploring small-town America.

Laura Leigh Strickland has been writing since she was seven years old, always eager to create something out of nothing. Laura writes stories and poems for her friends and family—her biggest fans. *Pay No Attention* is about sisters, built-in playmates and kindred spirits. She wrote it for Lyndsay and Haley.

Kim McClean Sullivan is a freelance writer as well as a columnist for a "Common Nonsense" for *The Coaster* newspaper. She lives in a small town in central New Jersey on the Jersey shore with her two sons, Kyle and Elijah, and their bunny rabbit, Thumper.

B. J. Taylor loves being a sister—there's nothing like it in the world! She is a *Guideposts* special correspondent/writer and has been published in numerous magazines, newspapers and many *Chicken Soup* books. B. J. is married to a wonderful man. They have four children and two adorable grandsons. You can reach B. J. through her Web site at *www.clik.to/bjtaylor.*

LeAnn Thieman, CSP, is a professional speaker, author and nurse, and the coauthor of seven *Chicken Soup for the Soul* books. To learn about her books, CDs, presentations and seminars, see *www.LeAnnThieman.com.*

Stephanie Welcher Thompson is a wife and stay-at-home mom who enjoys writing and scrapbooking when she's apart from husband, Michael, and their three-year-old daughter, Micah. She's a regular contributor to *Guideposts* and is blessed to be in four other *Chicken Soup* books. Reach her at P.O. Box 1502, Edmond, OK 73083 or *stephanie@stateofchange.net.*

Andrew Toos has established a national and international reputation through his off-beat lifestyle cartoons for clients such as *Reader's Digest, Saturday Evening Post, Gallery, Stern, Accountancy, Baseball Digest, CEO, The Washington Post, Barron's, Bayer Corp, Good Housekeeping, Cosmopolitan,* and many other titles and media outlets.

Joyce Tres lives in California with her husband and Siberian husky. A businesswoman, voracious reader, writer and artist, her poetry has been published in small publications. Currently she is working on three novels—a contemporary romance and two paranormal fantasies—and a collection of poetry. Reach Joyce at *Cabohemian@msn.com.*

Kristin Walker is a freelance writer and a stay-at-home mom. Her three sons constantly inspire her writing and her role as Fixer of All Things Smashed, Stained or Smelly. She lives happily with them and her husband in Oswego, Illinois.

L. J. Wardell is currently an earth scientist. She received her Ph.D. from the New Mexico Institute of Mining and Technology in 2002. She is a strong advocate of programs that assist women, minorities and the underprivileged in seeking higher education.

Luanna K. Warner holds an associate degree in photography and has been employed in the advertising industry for over twenty-five years as a copywriter.

She enjoys gardening, home improvement, creative writing and spending time with her family.

By profession, **Lois Wencil** is a writer. However, her true claim to fame is being mother, sister, volunteer and friend.

Susan Winslow spent ten years in advertising and now writes for an equine magazine. She lives on a horse farm with her husband, three children, and assorted horses, cats, dogs, chickens and a donkey. She enjoys photography, pottery and volunteering in therapeutic horseback riding. You can reach her by e-mail at *eastmeadowfarm@comcast.net*.

After spending fifteen years working with infants and toddlers in the art, music and dance field, **Robin Ehrlichman Woods** now spends her days writing about family, education and women's issues. Much of her inspiration is derived from childhood memories and the antics of her own children.

Our Memories, Moments and Must-Do's Together

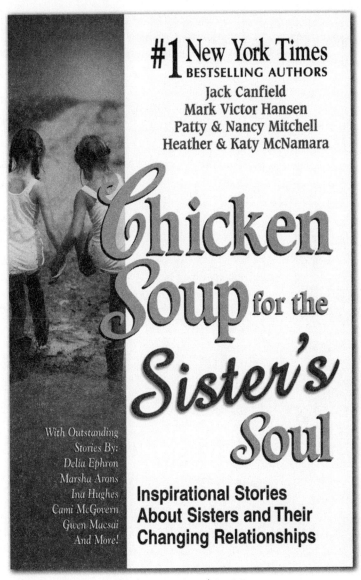

#1 New York Times
BESTSELLING AUTHORS
Jack Canfield
Mark Victor Hansen
Patty & Nancy Mitchell
Heather & Katy McNamara

Chicken Soup for the Sister's Soul

With Outstanding
Stories By:
Delia Ephron
Marsha Arons
Ina Hughes
Cami McGovern
Gwen Macsai
And More!

**Inspirational Stories
About Sisters and Their
Changing Relationships**

Code #0243 • $12.95

Take time for you.

Chicken Soup for the Breast Cancer Survivor's Soul

Stories to Inspire, Support and Heal

Jack Canfield, Mark Victor Hansen, and Mary Olsen Kelly

Code #5210 • $14.95

Chicken Soup for the Caregiver's Soul

Stories to Inspire Caregivers in the Home, Community and the World

Jack Canfield, Mark Victor Hansen and LeAnn Thieman, L.P.N.
with a Foreword by Rosalynn Carter

Code #1592 • $14.95

To order direct: Telephone (800) 441-5569 • www.hcibooks.com
Prices do not include shipping and handling. Your response code is CCS.

Also Available

Chicken Soup African American Soul
Chicken Soup African American Woman's Soul
Chicken Soup Breast Cancer Survivor's Soul
Chicken Soup Bride's Soul
Chicken Soup Caregiver's Soul
Chicken Soup Cat Lover's Soul
Chicken Soup Christian Family Soul
Chicken Soup College Soul
Chicken Soup Couple's Soul
Chicken Soup Dieter's Soul
Chicken Soup Dog Lover's Soul
Chicken Soup Entrepreneur's Soul
Chicken Soup Expectant Mother's Soul
Chicken Soup Father's Soul
Chicken Soup Fisherman's Soul
Chicken Soup Girlfriend's Soul
Chicken Soup Golden Soul
Chicken Soup Golfer's Soul, Vol. I, II
Chicken Soup Horse Lover's Soul, Vol. I, II
Chicken Soup Inspire a Woman's Soul
Chicken Soup Kid's Soul, Vol. I, II
Chicken Soup Mother's Soul, Vol. I, II
Chicken Soup Parent's Soul
Chicken Soup Pet Lover's Soul
Chicken Soup Preteen Soul, Vol. I, II
Chicken Soup Scrapbooker's Soul
Chicken Soup Sister's Soul, Vol. I, II
Chicken Soup Shopper's
Chicken Soup Soul, Vol. I-VI
Chicken Soup at Work
Chicken Soup Sports Fan's Soul
Chicken Soup Teenage Soul, Vol. I-IV
Chicken Soup Woman's Soul, Vol. I, II